DIANE FITZGERALD'S

SHAPED BEADWORK

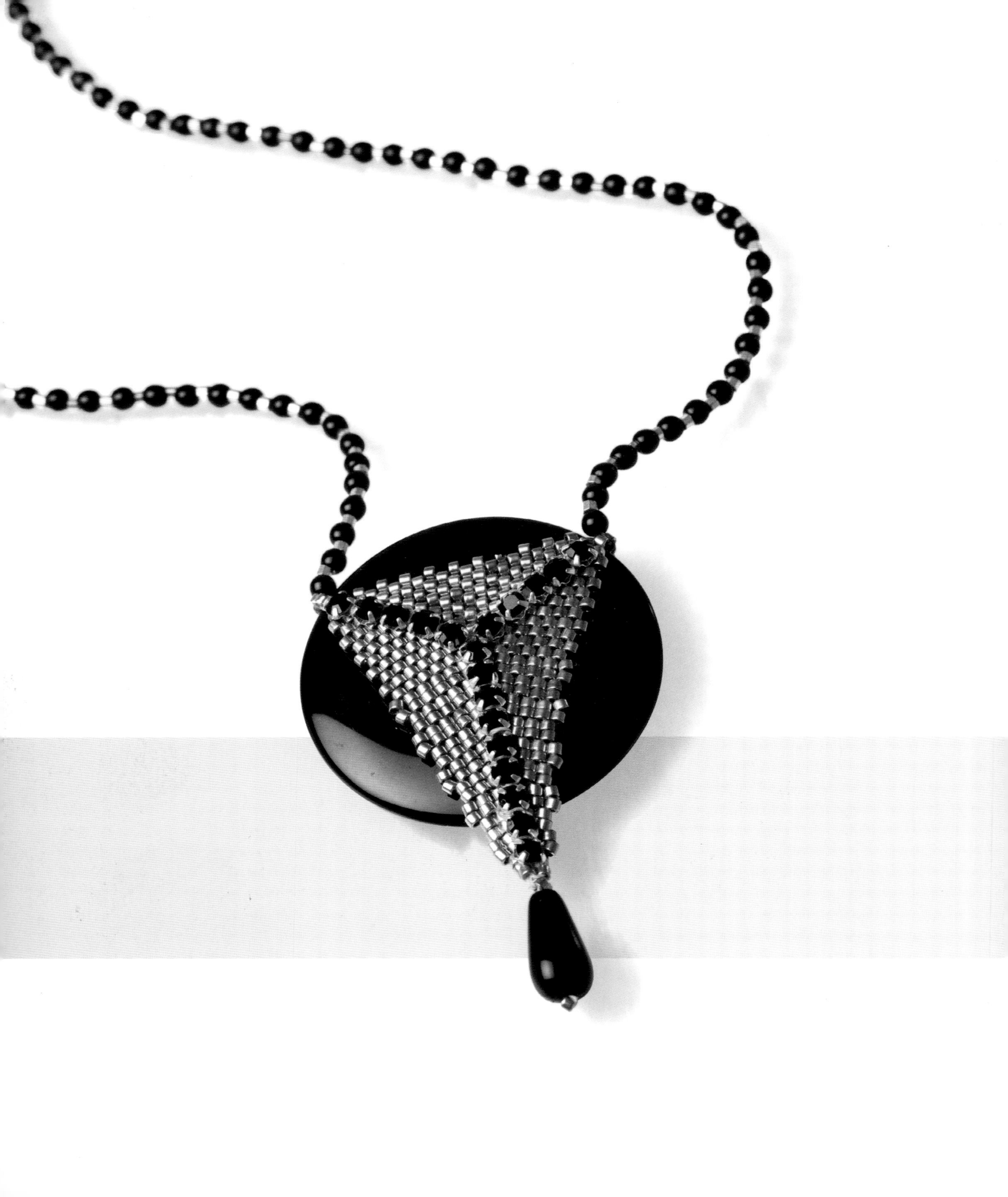

DIANE FITZGERALD

SHAPED BEADWORK
DIMENSIONAL JEWELRY WITH PEYOTE STITCH

LARK BOOKS

A Division of Sterling Publishing Co., Inc.
New York / London

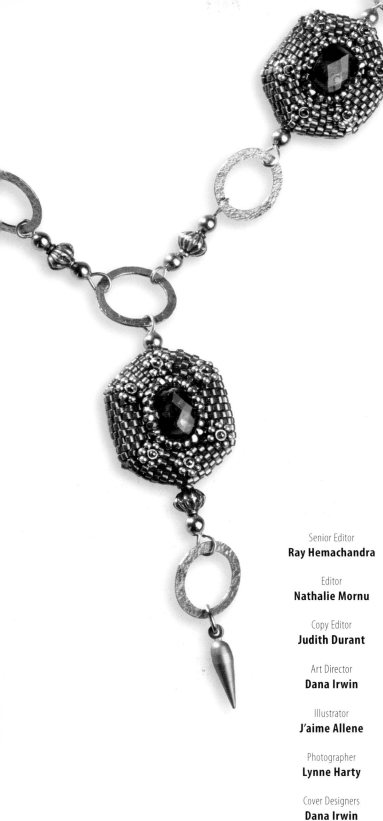

Senior Editor
Ray Hemachandra

Editor
Nathalie Mornu

Copy Editor
Judith Durant

Art Director
Dana Irwin

Illustrator
J'aime Allene

Photographer
Lynne Harty

Cover Designers
**Dana Irwin
Chris Bryant**

Library of Congress Cataloging-in-Publication Data

Fitzgerald, Diane.
   Diane Fitzgerald's shaped beadwork : dimensional jewelry with peyote stitch / Diane Fitzgerald. — 1st ed.
      p. cm.
   Includes bibliographical references and index.
   ISBN 978-1-60059-277-5 (hc-plc with jacket : alk. paper)
   1. Beadwork. 2. Beads. I. Title. II. Title: Shaped beadwork.
   TT860.F575 2009
   745.58'2--dc22

                              2008025703

10 9 8 7 6 5 4 3 2 1

First Edition

Published by Lark Books, A Division of
Sterling Publishing Co., Inc.
387 Park Avenue South, New York, NY 10016

Text © 2009, Diane Fitzgerald
Photography © 2009, Lark Books
Illustrations © 2009, Lark Books

Distributed in Canada by Sterling Publishing,
c/o Canadian Manda Group, 165 Dufferin Street
Toronto, Ontario, Canada M6K 3H6

Distributed in the United Kingdom by GMC Distribution Services,
Castle Place, 166 High Street, Lewes, East Sussex, England BN7 1XU

Distributed in Australia by Capricorn Link (Australia) Pty Ltd.,
P.O. Box 704, Windsor, NSW 2756 Australia

If you have questions or comments about this book, please contact:
Lark Books
67 Broadway
Asheville, NC 28801
828-253-0467

Manufactured in China

ISBN 13: 978-1-60059-277-5

For information about custom editions, special sales, and premium and corporate purchases, please contact the Sterling Special Sales Department at 800-805-5489 or specialsales@sterlingpub.com.

This book is dedicated to
Julia Pretl,
author of *Little Boxes,*
with many thanks
for the inspiration she offers in it.

**A golden lotus accents
the top of this large
purse, named Evening
in a Persian Garden.
It's constructed of four
triangles with free-form
designs, with a beaded
tassel dangling from the
bottom point.**

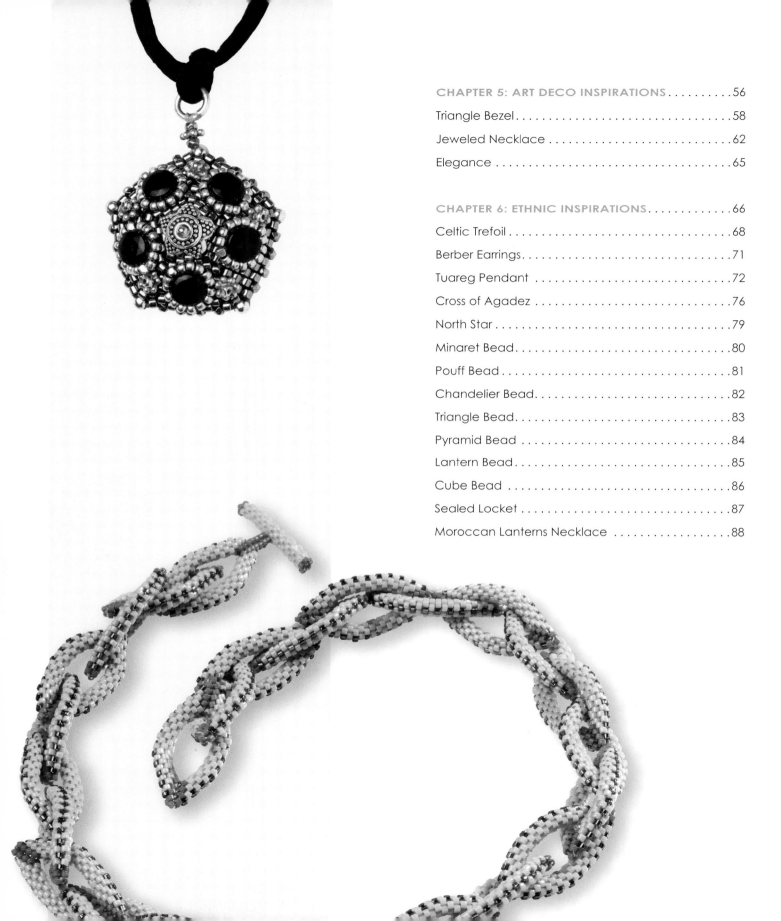

INTRODUCTION

SHAPES ANCIENT AND MODERN, NATURAL AND MAN-MADE, SURROUND US AND PROVIDE INSPIRATION FOR TODAY'S JEWELRY.

In the world of jewelry, shape is as important as color and sparkle and engages our minds as we study its rhythms. Focusing on shape will bring new creativity and excitement to your beadwork.

In this book I'll teach you to create geometric shapes—the triangle, the square, the pentagon, the hexagon, and many more—with peyote stitch. The shapes are made with specific patterns of increases that are easy to learn. Even though the shaping patterns described in this book are specific and precise, they're the building blocks of infinite magnificent designs in both two and three dimensions. They actually free you to be more creative, because you can better control what you do to make your work exactly as you envision it.

All the geometric shapes can be combined to create gorgeous, elegant jewelry, from earrings to brooches to bracelets. The Trillium Necklace on page 100 turns basic triangles into lovely flowers. The classic Tuareg Pendant (page 72) was inspired by metal ornaments worn in Mali. You can make a pair of Pointed Oval Links (page 92) to hang from ear wires or join a dozen or more to make a necklace. And the Moroccan Lanterns Necklace (page 88) combines the beaded-bead focal points of several other projects in the book to make a single, show-stopping piece of jewelry.

The supplies you'll need are simple: beading needles, nylon thread, and cylinder beads. You'll quickly be sculpting with beads and creating beautiful pieces of jewelry. I encourage you to begin by making the basic polygons—two-dimensional flat shapes—and to then progress to "donut" polygons, or two-dimensional shapes with holes in the center. Learning and practicing the increase patterns used to weave these shapes will prepare you for making three-dimensional shapes—polyhedrons—by combining the flat polygons in various ways.

I've spent close to three years specifically exploring shape in beadwork, and even now, more ideas tumble through my mind. I'm certain that you'll have great fun as you explore the creative possibilities. Let the geometric shapes inspire you to make original designs as you try shaping beadwork for yourself.

Diane M. Fitzgerald

CHAPTER ONE

BASICS

Tools and Supplies

Good beadwork starts with good beads, good thread, and a desire to make an appealing piece, whether it's a necklace, a bracelet, or an object. Here's a list of what you'll need to make the projects in this book. You'll always need a beading kit with basics such as needles, thread, and scissors. Specifics on bead requirements are listed with each project.

Basic Beading Kit

Beads

Size 11° cylinder beads are recommended for most of the techniques in this book. Two Japanese companies currently manufacture these: The Miyuki Company produces Delicas, and the Toho Company makes Aikos and Treasures.

Thread

I use nylon beading thread, and my favorite is Nymo D on the bobbin, which comes in a wide range of colors. Use it doubled for strength and durability, and wax the thread so the two strands stick together.

Needles

Beading needles come in various sizes and lengths. I use size 10 beading needles that are 2 inches (5.1 cm) long.

Scissors

A pair of small sharp scissors allows a clean thread cut, which in turn makes threading the needle much easier. Invest in good scissors and use them only for cutting thread; cutting paper or plastic will dull the blades.

Wax

Wax protects thread from abrasion and prevents tangling or knotting as you work. Choose synthetic or composition wax, the kind that comes in a cup; it maintains its stickiness for years. When working with doubled thread, draw the wax along the thread with the strands close together. Repeat until the strands adhere to each other.

Lighter

Use a lighter to slightly melt the knot at the end of your waxed thread and to singe short ends of thread that may be visible in your finished piece. See Securing Knots with a Lighter, on page 15.

Lighting

Always work in a well-lit space, preferably with the light coming from the left if you're right-handed or from the right if you're left-handed.

General Techniques

Lark's Head Knot

Most of the projects begin with a ring of beads secured with a lark's head or sales tag knot. Using this knot eliminates the need to weave in tails at the beginning of the work. Thread the needle, bring the thread ends together, and wax well. Knot the ends together with an overhand knot (figure 1). Clip the tails about 0.04 inch (1 mm) from the knot and melt the tails with a lighter (see below). String on the required number of beads and slide them to within 1 inch (2.5 cm) of the knot. Separate the strands between the knot and the beads. Pass the needle between the strands. Pull to form a ring. Don't allow the knot to slip into a bead. Pass back through the last bead strung (figure 2).

Securing Knots with a Lighter

With the thread tails extending from between the thumb and forefinger of your left hand, brace your left hand against your right hand. Flick the lighter and hold it down. Holding it straight up, slowly bring the thread tails toward the flame. Bring the end of the thread near, *not into*, the base of the flame, letting the heat melt the ends slightly. Don't let the thread sizzle, flare, or turn brown. Make certain the knot is secure by pulling on it with your thumbnail.

Adding Thread

There are many methods of adding thread; here's how I do it. Leave the old thread and needle connected to the beadwork to indicate where the new thread will be joined. When working with a double thread, if you knot both ends together, you may end up with a stubbly lump on the outside of your beadwork. To avoid this, thread your needle and tie an overhand knot in only one end of the thread. Melt the knot with a lighter. Pass the thread through two beads toward the bead where the old thread is exiting. Allow the knot to catch inside a bead. Pull the unknotted end through. Knot, clip, and melt the second tail. Draw the first and second threads through the beads until they exit the same bead as the old thread (figure 3). Tie the old thread and the new thread together with a square knot (figure 4) if you wish, or simply weave in the old thread and clip the tail.

Adding a Strand of Beads

With 1½ yd (1.4 m) of thread in the needle, bring the ends together, wax well, knot, clip the tail, and melt slightly. Attach one half of a clasp to the thread with a lark's head knot. String beads to desired length. Pass through a bead in the piece, then back through the strand of beads, around the clasp, and back through the last bead. Knot between the beads (figure 5), weave in the tail, and trim. Repeat for the other side.

figure 1
An overhand knot at the end of the new thread

figure 2

figure 3

figure 4
In a square knot, the left thread goes over the right thread and around it. The right thread then goes over the left thread and passes through the loop.

figure 5

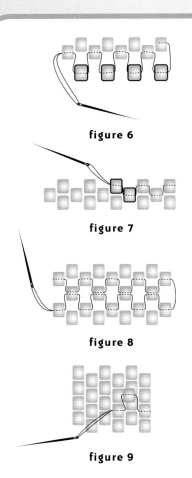

figure 6

figure 7

figure 8

figure 9

Peyote Stitch

Peyote describes a particular beadweaving technique. Generally it means to add a bead and then pass through the second bead in the previous row counting from where your thread exits a bead. In peyote stitch instructions, some beads are referred to as *up beads* and some as *down beads*. Up beads are in the previous row while down beads are in the row before that.

Basic Peyote Stitch

String the number of beads needed for the first row. Add one bead and pass through the second bead counting from where the thread exits a bead. Continue to add one bead and pass through the second bead (figure 6).

Circular and Tubular Peyote

When working peyote stitch in the round, increasing will make the beadwork lie flat. This is circular peyote. Working in the round without increasing will make the beadwork form a tube.

Peyote Step-Up

When working even-count circular or tubular peyote stitch you must pass through two beads at the end of each row to complete the row and move into position to begin the next row: the last bead of the previous row and the first bead added in the current row. The line of thread and the two beads outlined in figure 7 show a step-up.

Peyote Stitch Join
Zipping Edges with Connector Beads

To join two edges whose beads align bead-for-bead, work an extra row of peyote on one edge. These beads will be called *connector beads*. Align the pieces so the connector beads on one edge fit between the up beads on the other edge, then zip the edges together by weaving back and forth (figure 8).

Stitch in the Ditch

This quilting term means to quilt along a seam line. In beading, it means adding beads on top of a completed row of peyote stitch. To do it, exit a bead in the existing work, add a bead, and pass through the next bead of the row (figure 9).

Tips for Working the Projects

● Hold your work between your thumb and forefinger to keep it flat. Wrap the working thread over your forefinger and hold it in place with your middle finger. This helps keep the tension even and guides your eye to the next stitch.

● All instructions show the work progressing counter-clockwise (lefties, work clockwise).

● When working circular peyote, don't lose track of the step-up at the end of each row. If you've lost the step-up, undo the work until you locate the last correct step-up.

● When undoing the work, pull the eye of the needle through the bead.

● Check off your rows as you work so you don't lose your place.

● Keep the thread from tangling by untwisting it often.

● Throughout the book, A (Accent) beads, used for increases, are shown in terra cotta in the illustrations. B (Background) beads, used for the sides of a shape, are shown in blue. New beads for each row are shown with a bold line. Occasionally C (Connector) beads are also shown, in green.

● Once you're familiar with peyote stitch and the basics of the techniques in Chapter 2, you can use the Quick Reference on pages 110-112 for a handy refresher on making a Triangle, Square, Pentagon, or Hexagon.

Faux Bezel

A faux bezel is a ring of beads that surrounds a nailhead (flat-back bead) or a cabochon that's glued to a surface. The ring of beads is couched or stitched to the beadwork along the edge of the nailhead or cabochon. I use tiny glass or metal beads, size 15° or smaller.

With the thread exiting a bead near the edge of the nailhead or cabochon, string on enough beads to go around the nailhead or cabochon. Pass through the first three or four beads again. Tighten the ring and hold it in place. Stitch into the beadwork, passing through a bead if possible or around a thread between beads, then pass through the next few bezel beads. Connect the ring at four or five points, depending on the size of the nailhead or cabochon. To reinforce the bezel, pass through all the bezel beads again.

Toggle Closure

You may make a toggle closure with the pointed oval link or any of the open shapes on pages 33-39 by extending one tip or corner with square stitch and adding a peyote tube as the crossbar that will pass through another open shape.

1. Follow the instruction for your chosen open shape. On the final row, instead of adding 1 A bead to form a pointed tip or a corner, add 4 A beads. Pass back through the A bead next to the one you exited, then forward through the first A and through the first two A beads added in this step (figure 10).

2. Repeat step 1 by adding 4 more A beads (figure 11).

Repeat steps 1 and 2 for the other layer of the pointed oval or other shape.

For the toggle bar, make a piece of flat peyote 22 beads wide and 6 beads long. Zip the beginning and ending edges together to form a tube (see below). Sew the tube to the end of the square stitch extension. Sew back and forth to reinforce the connection.

figure 10

figure 11

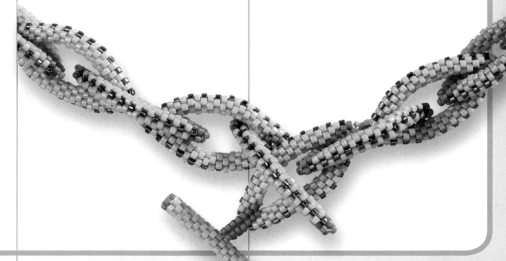

TWO-DIMENSIONAL SHAPES

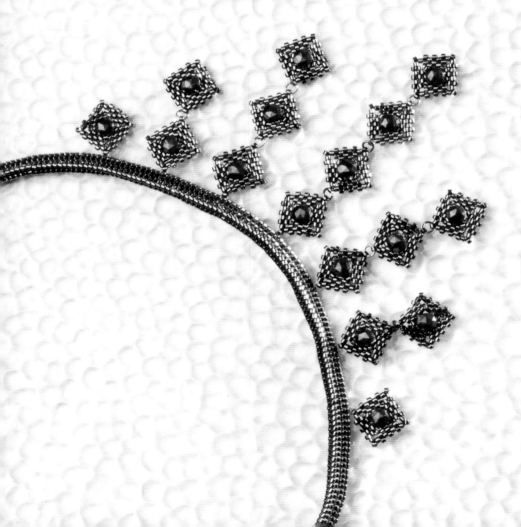

IN THIS CHAPTER YOU'LL LEARN to make the basic shapes upon which the projects are built. Practicing the triangle, square, pentagon, and hexagon increase patterns first will make your understanding of the rest of the book much easier. Size 11° cylinder beads in two colors are used for all the shapes: A for the Accent beads (increases) and B for the Background beads. *Note:* Peyote means to add a bead and pass through the second bead in the previous row counting from where your thread exits a bead.

figure 1

figure 2

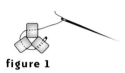

figure 3

figure 4

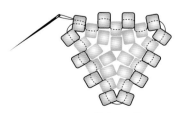

figure 5

Basic Triangle

This image shows the triangle worked with rows 1-4 and with a single bead at each corner in row 5, the final row.

With 1 yd (0.9 m) of thread in the needle, bring ends together, wax well, knot, clip the tail, and melt the ends slightly.

Row 1: Pick up 3 A and form a ring secured with a lark's head knot (figure 1).

Pass back through last bead strung (figure 2). Orient the work so you're working counter-clockwise (lefties, work clockwise).

Row 2: *Add 2 A and pass through the next A.* Repeat from * to * two more times. Step up (see page 16). These beads form the three corners of the triangle. Be sure the pairs of beads at each corner sit almost parallel. Adjust them if necessary (figure 3).

Row 3: *Add 2 A and pass through the next A.* Add 1 B and, skipping 1 bead in the row below, pass through the next A. Repeat from * to * two more times. Step up (figure 4).

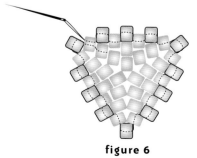

figure 6

Row 4: *Add 2 A and pass through the next A.* Peyote 2 with B. Repeat from * to * two more times. Step up (figure 5).

For a larger triangle, work additional rows like row 4 (peyote along the sides with B and add 2 A at each corner), then work the final row.

Final Row (Optional): Add only a 1 A at each corner instead of 2 A and peyote the sides with B (figure 6). Weave in the thread and trim.

Triangle Earrings with gold and black stripes

Silver Triangle Pin with channel-set stone embellishments and drop crystal pendant

Basic Square

This image shows a square worked with rows 1–6.

With 1 yd (0.9 m) of thread in the needle, bring ends together, wax well, knot, clip the tail, and melt the ends slightly.

Row 1: Pick up 4 A and form a ring secured with a lark's head knot (see page 15) as shown in figure 7.

Pass back through last bead strung (figure 8). These four beads form the corners of the square. Orient the work so you're working counter-clockwise (lefties, work clockwise).

Row 2: *Add 1 B and pass through the next A.* Repeat from * to * three more times. Step up (figure 9).

Row 3: *Add 3 A and pass through the next B.* Repeat from * to * three more times. Step up (figure 10). Be sure the middle bead of the three at each corner is pushed down as shown. If necessary, pull the outer beads apart and push the center bead down.

Row 4: *Add 2 A and pass through the third A of the set of three at the corner. Add 1 B and, skipping 1 B in the row below, pass through the next A.* Repeat from * to * three more times. Step up (figure 11).

Row 5: *Add 2 A and pass through the next A at this corner; peyote 2 with B.* Repeat from * to * three more times. Step up (figure 12).

figure 7

figure 8

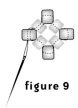

figure 9

figure 10

Row 6: *Add 1 A and pass through the next A at this corner; peyote 3 with B.* Repeat from * to * three more times. Step up (figure 13).

For a larger square, work rows 7-11.

Row 7: Peyote around with B. Step up (figure 14).

(continued on next page)

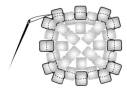

figure 11

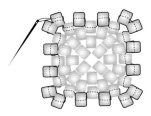

figure 12

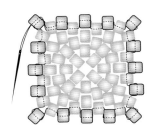

figure 13

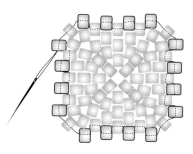

figure 14

21

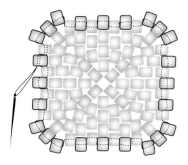

figure 15

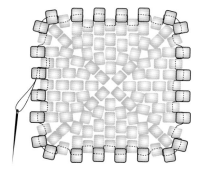

figure 16

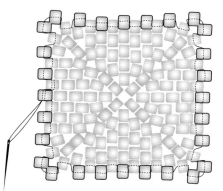

figure 17

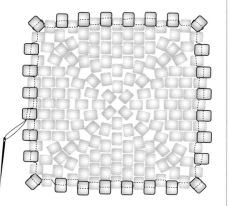

figure 18

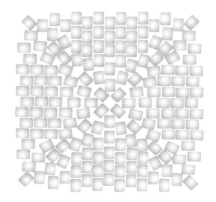

This image shows the square worked with rows 1-6 and with one repeat of rows 7-11.

Row 8: Add 3 A at each corner. (Be sure the center bead is pushed down as shown. If necessary, pull the outer beads apart and push the center bead down.) Peyote the sides with B. Step up (figure 15).

Row 9: Add 2 A at each corner and peyote the sides with B. Step up (figure 16).

Row 10: Add 2 A at each corner and peyote the sides with B. Step up (figure 17).

Row 11: Add 1 A at each corner and peyote the sides with B (figure 18). Weave in the thread and trim.

Necklace inspired by Turkoman temple pendants from Central Asia, made with squares worked Rows 1-6 and nailheads added. The squares are connected to a herringbone chain (page 114).

Basic Pentagon

This image shows a pentagon worked with rows 1-8.

With 2 yd (1.8 m) of thread in the needle, bring ends together, wax well, knot, clip the tail, and melt the ends slightly.

Row 1: Pick up 5 A and form a ring secured with a lark's head knot (see page 15). Pass back through the last bead strung. Orient the work so you're working counter-clockwise (lefties, work clockwise) as shown in figure 19.

Row 2: *Add 1 B and pass through the next A.* Repeat from * to * four more times. Step up (figure 20).

Row 3: *Add 2 A and pass through the next B.* Repeat from * to * four more times. Step up. Each pair of A beads forms a corner of the pentagon (figure 21).

Row 4: Add 1 A between the 2 A beads at each corner. Peyote the sides with B. Step up (figure 22).

Row 5: Peyote around with B. Step up (figure 23).

Row 6: *Peyote 1 with B. Add 3 A and pass through the next B.* Repeat from * to * four more times. Step up. Be sure the center bead is pushed down. If necessary, pull the outer beads apart and push the center

bead down (figure 24).

Row 7: Peyote 1 with B. *Add 2 A and pass through the third bead of the set of 3 A in the previous row. Peyote 2 with B.* Repeat from * to * four more times but on the last repeat peyote only 1. Step up (figure 25).

Row 8: Peyote 1 with B. *Add 1 A and pass through the next A. Peyote 3 with B.* Repeat from * to * four more times but on the last repeat peyote only 2 with B. Step up (figure 26).

For a larger pentagon, work rows 9-12.

Row 9: Peyote around with B.

Row 10: Peyote around with B but add 3 A at each corner.

Row 11: Peyote around with B but add 2 A at each corner as in row 7.

Row 12: Peyote around with B but add 1 A at each corner as in row 8.

Weave in the thread and trim.

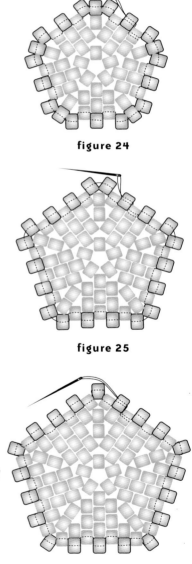

Star Locket variation
(See page 106)

figure 24

figure 25

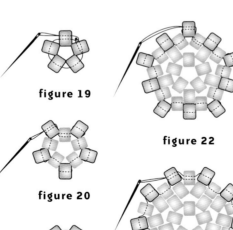

figure 19

figure 20

figure 21

figure 22

figure 23

figure 26

23

figure 27

figure 28

figure 29

figure 30

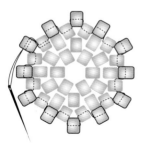

figure 31

Basic Hexagon

This image shows a hexagon worked with rows 1-8.

With 2 yd (1.8 m) of thread in the needle, bring ends together, wax well, knot, clip the tail, and melt the ends slightly.

Row 1: Pick up 6 A and form a ring secured with a lark's head knot (see page 15) as shown in figure 27. Pass back through the last bead strung. Orient the work so you're working counter-clockwise (lefties, work clockwise).

Row 2: *Add 1 A and pass through the next A.* Repeat from * to * five more times (figure 28). Step up. These A beads form the corners of the hexagon.

Row 3: Peyote around with B (figure 29). Step up.

Row 4: *Add 2 A and pass through the next B.* Repeat from * to * five more times (figure 30). Step up.

Row 5: Add 1 A between the 2 A at each corner and peyote the sides with B (figure 31). Step up.

Row 6: Peyote around with B.

Row 7: Peyote around with B but add 2 A at each corner.

Row 8: Peyote around with B but add 1 A at each corner.

For a larger hexagon, repeat rows 6-8.

Weave in the thread and trim.

Hexagon Bezel with Button.
A vintage button takes on new character with a hexagon bezel, fringes, and a strand of beads.

The pattern on the reverse side, above, makes the necklace reversible.

Elongated (Isosceles) Triangle

This image shows an isosceles triangle worked with rows 1-6 and row 7 as the final row.

This triangle has one extended point and resembles a stretched or elongated triangle. It has two equal sides and the third side is shorter than the other two.

With 1 yd (0.9 m) of thread in the needle, bring ends together, wax well, knot, clip the tail, and melt the ends slightly.

Row 1: Pick up 3 A and form a ring secured with a lark's head knot (see page 15). Pass back through the last bead strung. Orient the work so you're working counter-clockwise (lefties, work clockwise) (figure 32).

Row 2: Add 2 A and pass through the next A. Add 4 A and pass through the next bead. Add 2 A and pass through the next bead. Step up. These A beads form the corners of the triangle. Make certain the beads at each corner sit almost parallel. Adjust them if necessary (figure 33).

Row 3: Add 2 A and pass through the next corner A. Add 1 B and pass through the next 2 A. Add 4 A and pass through the next 2 A. Add 1 B and pass through 1 A. Add 2 A and pass through the next corner

bead. Add 1B and pass through the next A bead. Step up (figure 34).

Row 4: Add 2 A and pass through the next corner A. Add 1 B and pass through the next B. Add 2 B and pass through the next 2 A. Add 4 A and pass through the next 2 corner A. Add 2 B and pass through the next B. Add 1 B and pass through the next A. Add 2 A and pass through the next corner A. Peyote 2 with B. Step up (figure 35).

Subsequent Rows: Continue to add 2 A at the left and right corners and 4 A at the longer corner. Peyote the sides with B, adding 1 B above a single B and 2 B above the pairs of B.

Final Row: When the triangle is the desired size, work the final row with 1 A at the left and right corners and 3 A at the longer corner; peyote the sides with B. Weave in the thread and trim.

figure 32

figure 33

figure 34

figure 35

25

figure 36

figure 37

figure 38

figure 39

figure 40

Oval

This image shows the oval worked with rows 1-8.

Building on the Basic Hexagon shape, (page 24), we can make a flat oval.

With 2 yd (1.8 m) of thread in the needle, bring ends together, wax well, knot, clip the tail, and melt the ends slightly.

Row 1: Pick up 2 A and 3 B twice. Form a ring secured with a lark's head knot (see page 15). Pass back through the last B bead strung. Orient the work so you're working counter-clockwise (lefties, work clockwise) (figure 36).

Row 2: *Peyote 1 with B, peyote 3 with A.* Repeat from * to * once. Step up (figure 37).

Row 3: Peyote 8 with B. Step up (figure 38).

Row 4: *(Add 2 A and pass through the next B on the ring) three times, peyote 1 with B.* Repeat from * to * once. Step up (figure 39). The pairs of A beads form the six corners of the oval.

Row 5: Add 1 A between the 2 A beads at each corner and peyote the sides with B. Step up (figure 40).

Row 6: Peyote around with B. Step up.

Row 7: Peyote around with B but add 2 A at each corner. Step up.

The oval worked with rows 1-8 is apparent on the back of this locket (page 87).

Row 8: Peyote around with B but add 1 A between the 2 A beads at each corner. Step up.

For a larger oval repeat rows 6-8. Weave in the thread and trim.

Teardrop

This image shows the teardrop worked with rows 1-6 and row 7 as the final row.

Increase patterns may be combined to make more shapes, like this teardrop. Before working this shape, you should understand the triangle and hexagon increase patterns. Hold the work between your thumb and forefinger to maintain even tension and keep the piece flat.

With 2 yd (1.8 m) of thread in the needle, bring ends together, wax well, knot, clip the tail, and melt the ends slightly.

Row 1: Pick up 3 B, 3 A, 3 B and 2 A. Form a ring secured with a lark's head knot (see page 15). Pass back through the last A strung. Orient the work so you're working counter-clockwise (lefties, work clockwise) (figure 41).

Row 2: Add 2 A and pass through the next A. Peyote 2 with B. *Add 1 B and pass through the next A.* Repeat from * to * once. Peyote 2 with B. Step up (figure 42).

Row 3: Add 2 A and pass through the next A. Peyote 2 with B. *Add 2 A and pass through the next B.* Repeat from * to * twice. Peyote 2 with B. Step up (figure 43).

Row 4: Add 2 A and pass through the next A. Peyote 3 with B. *Add 1 A and pass

through the next A, then peyote 1 with B.* Repeat from * to * three times. Peyote 2 with B. Step up (figure 44).

Row 5: Add 2 A and pass through the next A. Peyote around with B. Step up.

Row 6: *Add 2 A and pass through the next A. Peyote 4 with B. *Add 2 A and pass through the next B, then peyote 3 with B.* Repeat from * to * three times. Step up.

Row 7: Add 2 A and pass through the next A. Peyote 5 with B. *Add 1 A and pass through the next A, then peyote 2 with B.* Repeat from * to * three times. Peyote 3 with B. Step up.

For a larger teardrop repeat rows 5-7. Continue to increase above the previous increases and peyote between these increases and along the sides.

Final Row: For a pointed end, add only one bead instead of two at the tip on the last row. Weave in the thread and trim.

Berber Earrings (page 71), shows the teardrop worked with rows 1-7.

figure 41

figure 42

figure 43

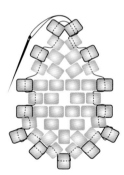

figure 44

figure 45

figure 46

figure 47

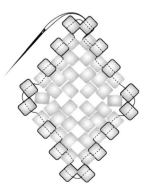

figure 48

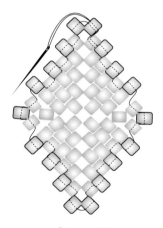

figure 49

Diamond

This image shows the diamond worked with rows 1-6 and one repeat of rows 3-6 with a single A bead at the north and south corners on the final row.

To make a diamond shape, two increase patterns are used: the triangle increase at the north and south corners and the hexagon increase at the east and west corners.

figure 50

Diamond Beads, (page 55), worked with rows 1-6.

With 2 yd (1.8 m) of thread in the needle, bring ends together, wax well, knot, clip the tail, and melt the ends slightly.

Row 1: Pick up 4 A beads and form a ring secured with a lark's head knot (see page 15). Pass back through the last bead strung (figure 45). Orient the work so you're working counter-clockwise (lefties, work clockwise)

Row 2: *Add 2 A and pass through the next A.* Repeat from * to * four times (figure 46). Step up. **Note:** The step-up will always occur at the same corner, the north corner.

Row 3: *Add 2 A and pass through the next A. Peyote 1 with B. Add 1 A and pass through the next A. Peyote 1 with B.* Repeat from * to * once. Step up. The corners with 2 A are the north and south corners and the corners with 1 A are the east and west corners (figure 47).

Row 4: Add 2 A and pass through the next A at the north and south corners. Peyote the sides with B, passing through the A beads at the east and west corners (figure 48). Step up.

Row 5: Add 2 A and pass through the next A at the north and south corners. Peyote the sides with B. At the east and west corners, add 2 A (above the A) and pass through the next B (figure 49). Step up.

Row 6: Add 2 A and pass through the next A at the north and south corners. Peyote the sides with B. At the east and west corners, add 1 A and pass through the next A. Step up (figure 50).

For a larger diamond, repeat rows 3-6.

Final Row: Add single beads at the north and south corners only on the final row. Weave in the thread and trim.

Rectangle

This image shows the rectangle worked with rows 1-5.

To make a rectangle, which is really an elongated square, use the increase pattern for the square and extend two opposite sides.

With 2 yd (1.8 m) of thread in the needle, bring ends together, wax well, knot, clip the tail, and melt the ends slightly.

Row 1: Pick up 7 B, 1 A, 1 B and 1 A twice. Form a ring secured with a lark's head knot (see page 15). Pass back through the last bead strung (figure 51). Orient the work so you're working counter-clockwise (lefties, work clockwise).

Row 2: *Peyote 3 with B. Add 3 A and pass through the next B two times.* Repeat from * to * once. Make certain the center bead is pushed down as shown. If necessary, pull the outer beads apart and push the center bead down. Step up (figure 52).

Row 3: Peyote the sides with B, and at each corner add 2 A and pass through the third A of the set of three at the corner. Step up (figure 53).

Row 4: Peyote the sides with B, and at each corner add 2 A and pass through the next A. Step up (figure 54).

Row 5: Peyote the sides with B, and at each corner add 1 A and pass through the next A. Step up (figure 55).

For a larger rectangle, repeat rows 7-11 of the basic square. If desired, fill in the center with a row of peyote stitch. Weave in the thread and trim

The Rectangle, worked rows 1-5, is used in the Tuareg Pendant (page 72).

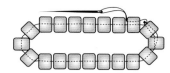

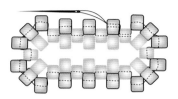

figure 51

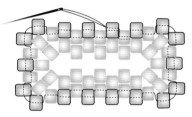

figure 52

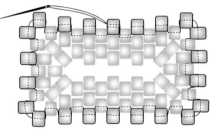

figure 53

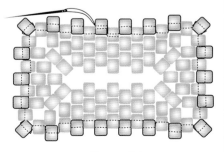

figure 54

figure 55

CHAPTER THREE

OPEN SHAPES

USE THESE OPEN SHAPES TO MAKE BRACELET CHARMS, EARRINGS, TOGGLE CLASPS, OR LINKS IN A CHAIN.

The shapes have two layers and you may use different colors on each side. To make them larger, increase the number of B (Background) beads on each side in the first row (increase to an uneven number of beads) and adjust the pattern accordingly. After completing the shape, you may add a closed ring or a loop of beads to attach to a bracelet or earring finding.

Basic Instructions

Use size 11° cylinder beads and even-count circular peyote stitch with a step-up at the end of each row (see page 16) for all ten shapes. Begin each shape with a ring of the specified number of beads using A for the corner increases and B for the sides. After working the first layer, pass back to the first row of beads and work the second layer like the first layer. Finally, zip the two layers together along the outer edge (see page 16). All the shapes are about 1 inch (2.5 cm) long.

Prepare the Thread

With 2 yd (1.8 m) of thread in the needle, bring the ends together, wax well, knot, and clip the tails, and melt them slightly with a lighter.

Form the Beginning Ring

Pick up the beads for row 1 and form a ring secured with a lark's head knot (see page 15). Orient the work so you're working counterclockwise (lefties, work clockwise). Hold the work between your thumb and forefinger to keep it flat and work with medium tension.

Bead the Shapes

Please see the Basics chapter, including how to do circular peyote stitch, forming the beginning ring with a lark's head knot, working the step-up at the end of a row, and zipping edges together.

The Open Shapes. Clockwise from bottom left: rectangle, triangle, teardrop, pentagon, hexagon, square, elongated (isosceles) triangle, pointed oval, diamond, and oval

Peyote means to add a bead and pass through the second bead in the previous row counting from where the thread exits a bead.

Pass through means to pass the needle forward in the direction of the work.

Pass back through means to pass the needle back through the last bead in the opposite direction of the previous pass.

SUPPLIES FOR ONE CHARM

Basic Beading Kit
    (see page 14)

Size 11° cylinder beads:
    color A, 1 g
    color B, 2 g

Open Triangle

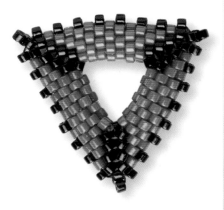

First Layer

Row 1: Pick up 1 A and 7 B three times. Form a ring secured with a lark's head knot (see page 15). Pass back through last bead strung (figure 1).

Row 2: Peyote the sides with B but add 2 A over the A at each corner. Step up (figure 2). **Note:** The step-up will move for each row.

Rows 3-5: Peyote the sides with B; after exiting the A at each corner, add 2 A and pass through the next A. Don't skip a bead. Step up.

Row 6: Peyote the sides with B but add only 1 A between the pair of A beads at each corner (figure 3). Pass through the beads so the thread exits the down bead marked X in figure 3. There should be four pairs of beads at each corner increase.

Second Layer

Work this layer from the down beads in the first row, the row closest to the center.

Row 1: Peyote around with B, passing through the A at each corner. Push the new beads toward the outer edge of the first layer.

Row 2: Repeat Row 2 of the first layer.

Rows 3-5: Repeat Row 3 of the first layer 3 times.

Zip the second layer to the first layer (see page 16). At each corner, pass through the first A at the corner of the second layer, then through the single A at the corner of the first layer, and then through the second A of the second layer. Weave in the thread and trim.

Open Elongated (Isosceles) Triangle

Work this shape like the open triangle but with additional beads on two opposite sides.

Row 1: Pick up 1 A, 11 B, 1 A, 5 B, 1 A, 11 B.

Follow the instructions for the open triangle, adjusting the number of beads. To make this shape larger, increase the number of beads by two on each side. For example, row 1 could have 1 A, 15 B, 1 A, 7 B, 1 A, 15 B.

Open Triangle Earrings suspended by decorative necklace backbars

figure 1

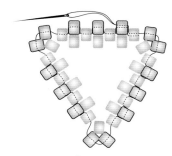

figure 2

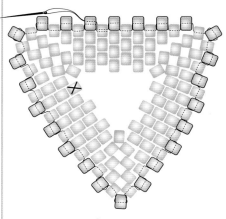

figure 3

Open Square

First Layer

Row 1: Pick up 1 A and 5 B four times. Form a ring secured with a lark's head knot (see page 15). Pass back through the last bead strung (figure 1).

Row 2: Peyote the sides with B but add 3 A at each corner. Make certain the middle A of each set of three A is pushed down so it's parallel with the bead in the row below. Step up (figure 2).

Row 3: Peyote the sides with B and at each corner, exit the first A, add 2 A and pass through the third A (figure 3). Step up.

Row 4: Peyote the sides with B but at each corner add 2 A between the pair of A beads. Step up (figure 4).

Row 5: Peyote around with B but at each corner add 1 A between the pair of A beads (figure 5).

Pass through the beads to the first row so the thread exits a down bead closest to the center.

Second Layer

Work the second layer from the first row of down beads in the first layer.

Row 1: Peyote around with B passing

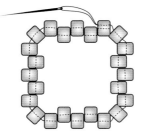

figure 1

figure 2

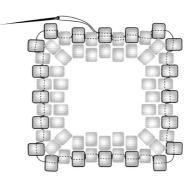

figure 3

through the A beads at each corner. Push the new beads toward the outer edge of the first layer.

Rows 2-4: Repeat rows 2-4 of the first layer.

Zip the second layer to the first layer (see page 16). At each corner, pass through the first A at the corner of the second layer, then through the single A at the corner of the first layer, and then through the second A of the second layer.

Weave in the thread and trim.

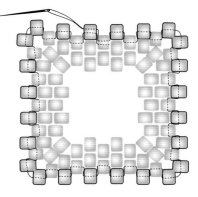

figure 4

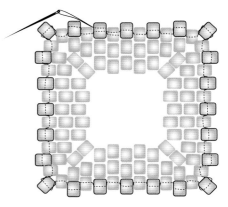

figure 5

Open Rectangle

Work the open rectangle like the open square (page 34) but add more beads on the two opposite sides.

Row 1: Pick up 1 A, 5 B, 1 A, 9 B twice.

Follow the instructions for the square, adjusting the number of beads. To make this bead larger, increase the number of beads by two on opposite sides.

Open Pentagon

First Layer

Row 1: Pick up 1 A and 3 B five times. Form a ring secured with a lark's head knot (see page 15). Pass back through the last bead strung (figure 1).

Row 2: *Peyote 1 with B but add 2 A above the A.* Repeat from * to * four more times. Step up (figure 2).

Row 3: Peyote the sides with B but add 1 A between the pair of A beads at each corner. Step up (figure 3).

Row 4: Peyote around with B. Step up (figure 4).

Row 5: Peyote around with B but add 3 A above each A. Step up (figure 5). Make certain the middle A of each set of three A beads is pushed down so it's parallel with the bead in the row below.

Row 6: Peyote around with B but after exiting the first A in the set of three at each corner, add 2 A, then pass through the third A of that set. Step up (figure 6).

Row 7: Peyote around with B but add 1 A between the pair of A beads at each corner.

Pass through the beads to the first row so the thread exits a down bead closest to the center (figure 7).

Second Layer

Work the second layer from the first row of down beads in the first layer.

Row 1: Peyote around with B passing through the A at each corner. Push the new beads toward the outer edge of the first layer.

Rows 2-6: Repeat Rows 2-6 of the first layer.

Zip the second layer to the first layer (see page 16). At each corner, pass through the first A at the corner of the second layer, then through the single A at the corner of the first layer, and then through the second A of the second layer. Weave in the thread and trim.

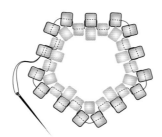

figure 1

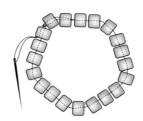

figure 2

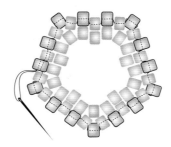

figure 3

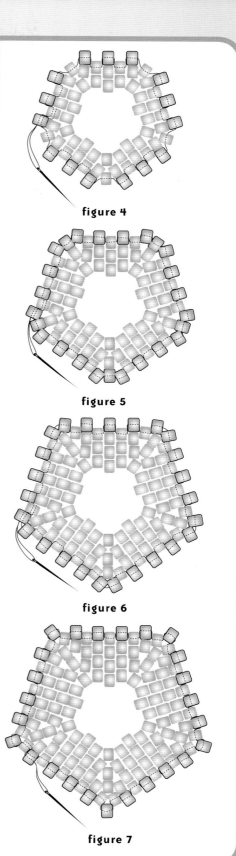

figure 4

figure 5

figure 6

figure 7

Open Hexagon

First Layer

Row 1: Pick up 1 A and 3 B six times. Form a ring secured with a lark's head knot (see page 15). Pass back through the last bead strung (figure 1).

Row 2: Peyote the sides with B but add 2 A above each A. Step up (figure 2).

Row 3: Peyote the sides with B but add 1 A between the pair of A beads at each corner. Step up (figure 3).

Row 4: Peyote around with B. Step up (figure 4).

Rows 5-6: Repeat rows 2-3.

Pass through the beads to the first row so the thread exits a down bead closest to the center.

Second Layer

Work the second layer from the first row of down beads in the first layer.

Row 1: Peyote around with B, passing through the A beads at each corner. Push the new beads toward the outer edge of the first layer.

Rows 2-5: Repeat rows 2-5 of the first layer.

Zip the second layer to the first layer (see page 16). At each corner, pass through the first A at the corner of the second layer, then through the single A at the corner of the first layer, and then through the second A of the second layer. Weave in the thread and trim.

Double Open Hexagon Earrings

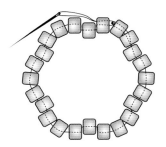

figure 1

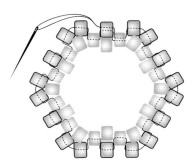

figure 2

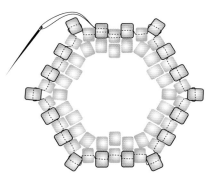

figure 3

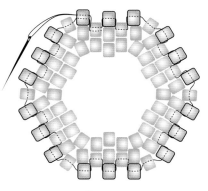

figure 4

Open Oval

Work the open oval like the open hexagon but add more beads on two opposite sides.

Row 1: Pick up 1 A and 3 B six times. Form a ring secured with a lark's head knot (see page 15). Pass back through the last bead strung (figure 1).

Follow the instructions for the open hexagon, (page 36), adjusting the number of beads.

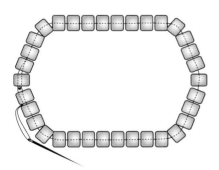

figure 1

Open Teardrop

Make the open teardrop with the triangle increase pattern at the top point and the hexagon increase pattern for the three bottom points.

First Layer

Row 1: Pick up 1 A, 11 B, 1 A, 3 B, 1 A, 3 B, 1 A, 11 B. Form a ring secured with a lark's head knot (see page 15). Pass back through the last bead strung (figure 1).

Row 2: Peyote 5 with B, add 2 A above the A, peyote 1 with B, add 2 A above the A, peyote 1 with B, add 2 A above the A, peyote 5 with B, add 2 A above the A. Step up (figure 2).

Row 3: Peyote 5 with B, add 1 A between the pair of A beads, peyote 2 with B, add 1 A between the pair of A beads, peyote 2 with B, add 1 A between the pair of A beads, peyote 6 with B, add 2 A between the pair of A beads, peyote 1 with B. Step up (figure 3).

(continued on next page)

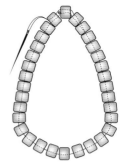

figure 1

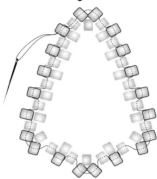

figure 2

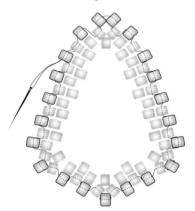

figure 3

Bracelet of open and closed shapes

37

figure 4

figure 5

figure 6

Row 4: Peyote 18 with B, add 2 A between the pair of A beads, peyote 2 with B. Step up (figure 4).

Row 5: Peyote 4 with B, add 2 A above the A, peyote 2 with B, add 2 A above the A, peyote 7 with B, add 2 A above the A, peyote 3 with B. Step up (figure 5).

Row 6: Peyote 4 with B, add 1 A between the pair of A beads, peyote 3 with B, add 1 A between the pair of A beads, peyote 3 with B, add 1 A between the pair of A beads, peyote 8 with B, add 1 A between the pair of A beads, peyote 4 with B (figure 6).

Pass through the beads to the first row so the thread exits a down bead closest to the center.

Second Layer

Work the second layer from the first row of down beads in the first layer.

Row 1: Peyote around with B passing through the A beads. Step up.

Rows 2-5: Repeat rows 2-5 of the first layer.

Zip the second layer to the first layer (see page 16). At each corner, pass through the first A at the corner of the second layer, then through the single A at the corner of the first layer, and then through the second A of the second layer. Weave in the thread and trim.

Open Pointed Oval

The open pointed oval is made like the open triangle (page 33) but with only two sides instead of three.

Row 1: Pick up 1 A and 7 B twice.

Follow the instructions for the open triangle, working only two sides.

Open Diamond

First Layer

Make the open diamond with the triangle increase at the north and south corners and the hexagon increase at the east and west corners.

Row 1: Pick up 1 A and 7 B four times. Form a ring secured with a lark's head knot. Pass back through the last bead strung (figure 1).

Row 2: Peyote the sides with B but add 2 A at each corner. Step up (figure 2).

Row 3: Peyote the sides with B but add 2 A at the north and south corners and 1 A at the east and west corners. Step up (figure 3).

Row 4: Peyote the sides with B but add 2 A at the north and south corners, pass through the A beads at the east and west corners. Step up (figure 4).

Row 5: Peyote the sides with B but add 2 A at all four corners. Step up (figure 5).

Row 6: Peyote the sides with B but add 1 A between the pair of A beads at each corner. Step up (figure 6).

Pass through the beads to the first row so the thread exits a down bead closest to the center.

Second Layer

Work the second layer from the first row of down beads in the first layer.

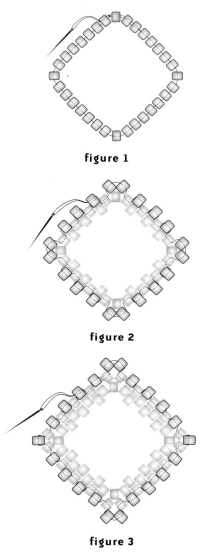

figure 1

figure 2

figure 3

Row 1: Peyote around with B, passing through the A beads at each corner. Push the new beads toward the outer edge of the first layer.

Rows 2-5: Repeat rows 2-5 of the first layer.

Zip the second layer to the first layer (see page 16). At each corner, pass through the first A at the corner of the second layer, then through the single A at the corner of the first layer, and then through the second A of the second layer. Weave in the thread and trim.

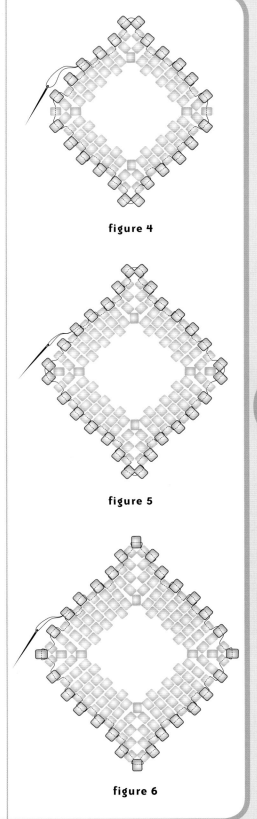

figure 4

figure 5

figure 6

CHAPTER FOUR

THREE-DIMENSIONAL SHAPES

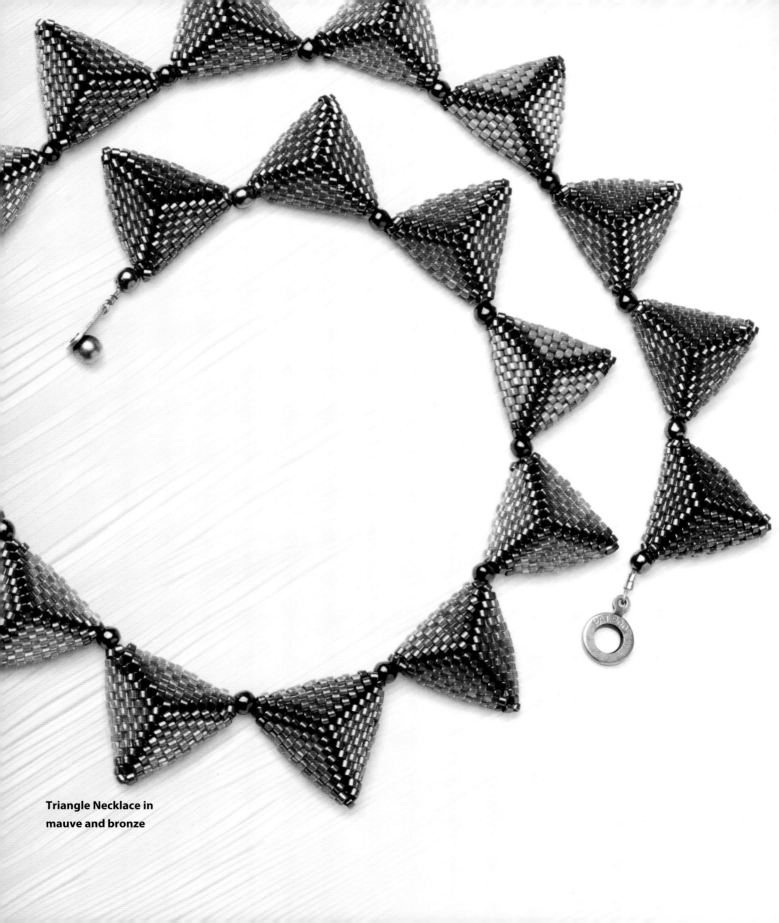

**Triangle Necklace in
mauve and bronze**

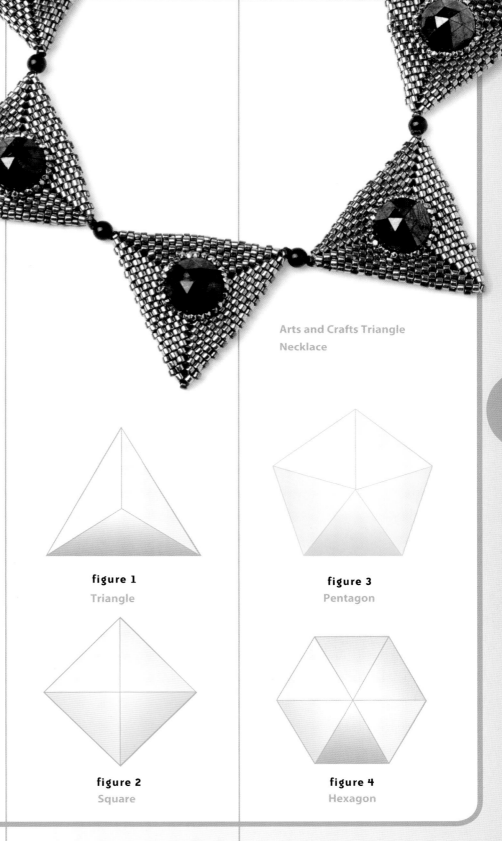

Increase Patterns

IN THIS CHAPTER YOU'LL LEARN

to use increase patterns to create three-dimensional shapes. For example, to create a pyramid shape, use the pentagon increase pattern with four sides instead of five. To create a shallow domed pentagon, use the hexagon increase pattern with five sides instead of six.

It's easiest to see this with a paper model. Photocopy and enlarge these four shapes (figures 1-4) and cut them out. Fold the shapes along the radiating lines. Next, cut one of the lines from the corner to the center and overlap two of the sections. The flat shape becomes domed. Interesting new shapes can also be made by adding a section.

Arts and Crafts Triangle Necklace

figure 1
Triangle

figure 3
Pentagon

figure 2
Square

figure 4
Hexagon

Memphis Earrings

Two-Layer Triangle Earrings
in green and magenta

Two-Layered Triangle

Begin by making a Basic Triangle with one bead at each corner on the last row (see page 20). Make a second triangle with one less row and two beads at each corner. Zip the two triangles together (see page 16). For a decorative edge, use size 8° Czech drops for the connector beads in the last row of the first triangle.

**Orange and Blue
Triangle Necklace**

Tetra Bead Necklace

Tetra Bead

**The bead shown measures ½ inch
(1.3 cm)**

A Tetra Bead is a three-dimensional
pyramid with three triangular sides and
a triangular base. Sizes can range from ½
inch (1.3 cm) to 1 inch (2.5 cm) or larger.
Instructions are for a ½-inch (1.3 cm) bead.
String finished beads together corner to
corner or corner to side.

Side Triangles

Make three triangles working rows 1-4 of
the Basic Triangle (see page 24). For row
5 add only 1 A at each corner instead of 2.
There should be 3 B beads sticking up on
each side with 1 A at each corner. Weave
in the thread and clip.

SUPPLIES

**Basic Beading Kit
(see page 14)**

Size 11° cylinder beads:
    color A, 2 g
    color B, 2 g

Tetra Beads in various color patterns

Base Triangle

Begin with 2 yd (1.8 m) of thread. This is enough thread to make the base and weave the triangles together. Complete a triangle as above for the sides. Add a row of connector beads with B on all three sides (shown with a bold outline in figure 1), passing through the single corner beads without adding beads. End with the thread exiting a corner bead. Don't knot or cut the thread.

Assemble the Triangles

1. Join one triangle to each side of the base, weaving back and forth from the connector beads on the base to the side of a triangle and passing through the corner beads of the base triangle (figure 2).

2. Pass through the beads as shown in figure 3 so the thread exits an outer corner bead.

3. Add 4 connector beads with B (shown in figure 4 with a bold outline) to one side of the triangle. Pass through the corner beads of the next three triangles (figure 4).

4. Pass through the corner beads a second time, pull to tighten, then zip the triangle on the left to the connector beads of the triangle on the right (figures 5 and 6). Repeat steps 3 and 4 for the remaining sides. After the three sides are zipped together, pass through the last three corner beads a second time. Weave in the thread and trim.

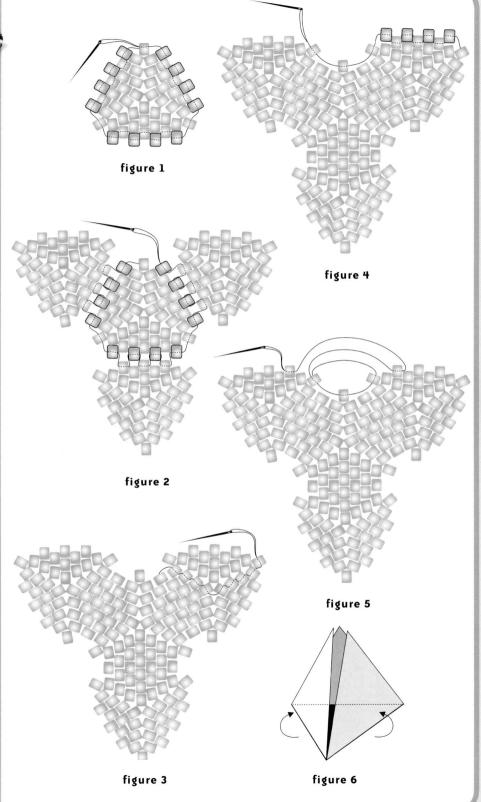

figure 1

figure 2

figure 3

figure 4

figure 5

figure 6

figure 1

figure 2

figure 3

figure 4

Cube Bead

The bead shown measures ½ inch (1.3 cm).

A Cube Bead is a three-dimensional shape with six square sides. Instructions are for a ½-inch (1.3 cm) bead. String finished cube beads corner to corner or side to side.

Side Squares

Make five squares following the directions for the Basic Square (see page 25), working through row 6. (For a larger square, work through row 11 and adjust the following instructions accordingly.)

Base Square

Begin with 2 yd (1.8 m) of thread. This is enough to make the base square and weave the squares together. Complete a square as described above for the sides. Weave through the beads so the thread exits a corner bead. Add a row of connector beads with B, passing through the single corner beads without adding beads (figure 1).

SUPPLIES

**Basic Beading Kit
(see page 14)**

**Size 11° cylinder beads:
color A, 2 g
color B, 2 g**

Cube Earrings worked with rows 1-6

Assemble the Squares

1. Join one square to each side of the base. Weave back and forth from the connector beads on one side of the base to the side of a square. Pass through the corner bead and the first connector bead of the base square, then add the next square. Repeat this step for the remaining sides (figure 2).

2. Pass through the three corner beads so the thread exits to the left from the upper right corner bead of the top square. See the arrow in figure 3.

3. Peyote 4 with B along the top side of the square, pass through the corner bead, then peyote 4 with B along the left side of the square. End with the thread exiting the bottom left corner (figure 3). Pass through the corner bead of the base square, then the corner bead of the next square to the left. Pass through the three corner beads again.

4. Weave back and forth to connect the sides as shown in figure 4.

Repeat steps 3 and 4 for the remaining three sides. Don't cut the thread.

Add the Final Square

Connector beads are already in place to add the sixth side. Join the last square by weaving back and forth between the sides of this square and the connector beads on the sides of the cube. Weave in the thread and trim.

Dodeca Bead

This Dodeca Bead is 1¼ inches (3.2 cm) in diameter.

A Dodeca Bead is a three-dimensional spherical shape composed of 12 pentagons (five-sided flat shapes) joined with connector beads. It may be easier to think of it as two bowls joined together, one upright and one inverted. Each bowl is made of six pentagons, one for the base and one added to each side of the base as shown in figure 1.

Instructions are for a 1¼-inch (3.2 cm) bead.

First Half

1. Side Pentagons

Make five pentagons following the instructions for the Basic Pentagon (page 23), working through row 8. Weave in the thread and trim.

2. Base Pentagon

Begin with 2 yd (1.8 m) of thread. This is enough to make the base and weave the pentagons together. Complete a pentagon as described in step 1. Weave the thread through the beads so it exits a corner bead. Don't tie off the thread.

3. Join the Pentagons

A. Peyote around the base pentagon with B adding 4 beads to each side and pass-

SUPPLIES

Basic Beading Kit
   (see page 14)

Size 11° cylinder beads:
   color A, 4 g (these form the
spokes of each pentagon)
   color B, 4 g

ing through the corner A beads. The 4 beads added on each side are connector beads.

B. Weave back and forth from the connector beads on the base pentagon to the beads on one side of the first pentagon. At the corner of the base, continue clockwise and pass through the corner bead and the next connector bead (figure 2). Repeat this step for the remaining four sides.

C. Weave through the beads so the thread exits a corner bead of one pentagon, indicated with an arrow in figure 3. Peyote along three sides of the pentagon with B. The beads added along the first and second sides are connector beads that'll be used to join the second half of the beaded bead to the first half. You'll use the beads added to the third side to join this side to the side of the next pentagon as shown in figure 3. Repeat for the remaining pentagons. Weave in the thread and trim.

Second Half

Make six more pentagons and join as described for the first half through joining step B. For step C, don't add the beads along the outer edge of each pentagon.

(continued on next page)

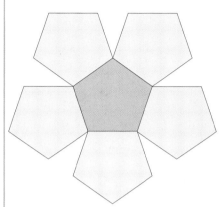

figure 1

figure 2

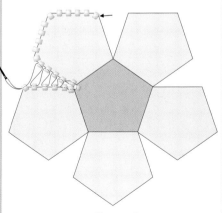

figure 3

49

Rainbow Dodeca Bead

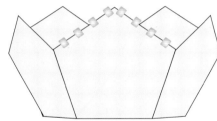

figure 4

(The connector beads have already been added to the first half.) Instead, just pass the through beads to the next corner, add the connector beads, and weave the sides together. Repeat for the remaining pentagons.

Join the Bead Halves

Join the first half of the bead to the second half, weaving between the outer beads of the second half and the row of connector beads of the first half. The point of one pentagon should fit into the corner formed by two pentagons in the other half (figure 4).

Weave in the thread and trim. To stiffen the bead, dip it in acrylic floor polish, blot excess liquid with a tissue, and let it dry on waxed paper.

Vessel or Bowl

To make a vessel or bowl, work only through Step 3C of the Dodeca Bead. Then, working from the connector beads around the base pentagon, add four rows of peyote stitch with a size 6 drop bead at each corner in the last row.

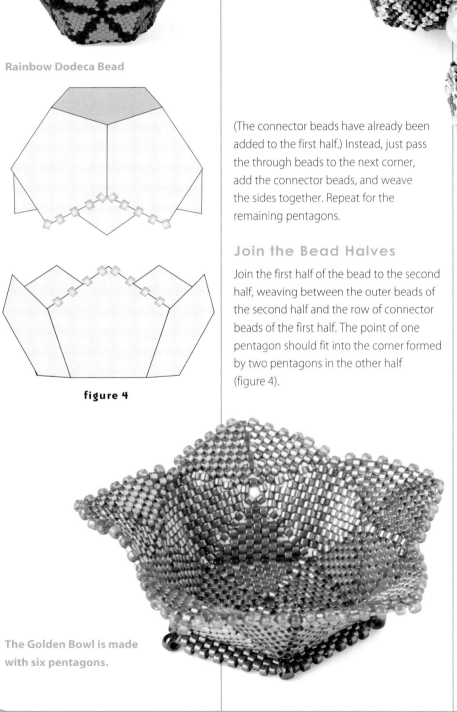

The Golden Bowl is made with six pentagons.

Octa Bead

SUPPLIES

Basic Beading Kit
   (see page 14)

Size 11° cylinder beads:
   color A, 1 g
   color B, 2 g

An Octa Bead has eight triangular sides and looks like two four-sided pyramids with their bases joined. Octa Beads are made like the Deca Bead but with four sides instead of five. Sizes may range from ¾ inch (2 cm) to 1 inch (2.5 cm) or larger. Instructions are for a 1-inch (2.5 cm) bead. String finished beads end to end.

First Half

With 2 yd (1.8 m) of thread in the needle, bring the ends together, wax well, knot, clip the tail, and melt the ends slightly.

Row 1: Pick up 4 A and form a ring secured with a lark's head knot (see page 15). Pass back through the last bead strung.

Row 2: *Add 1 A and pass through the next A (don't skip a bead).* Repeat from * to * three more times. Step up. These beads form the corners.

Row 3: Peyote around with B. Step up. Pull the thread tight so the piece begins to form a cup.

Row 4: Add 2 A at each corner.

Note: On subsequent repeats of this row, peyote between the corners with B. Step up.

Row 5: Peyote around with B and add 1 A between the 2 A beads at each corner. Step up.

Rows 6-17: Repeat rows 3-5 four more times. There'll be a single A at each corner and 5 B sticking up on each side between the corner A beads. Weave in the thread and trim.

Second Half

Work through row 17 as for the first half but don't knot or cut the thread.

Row 18: Peyote around with A. These beads are the connector beads.

Join the Two Halves

Align the corners and weave back and forth between the two halves around the bead, zipping the two edges together (see page 16). Weave in the thread and trim.

Five Dodeca Beads Necklace

This necklace includes an Octa Bead, Deca Bead, Tetra Bead, Cube Bead, and Dodeca Bead.

Deca Bead

A Deca Bead is a hollow disk-like bead with 10 triangular sides. Some people call it the Flying Saucer bead. Deca Beads are made in two halves using circular, even-count peyote stitch with the hexagon increase pattern but with only five sides instead of six. These instructions are for a ½-inch (1.3 cm) bead that's 1 inch (2.5 cm) in diameter. String finished beads end to end or suspend them from a corner.

First Half

With 2 yd (1.8 m) of thread in the needle, bring the ends together, wax well, knot, clip the tail, and melt the ends slightly.

Row 1: Pick up 5 A and form a ring secured with a lark's head knot (see page 15). Pass back through the last bead strung.

Row 2: *Add 1 A and pass through the next A (don't skip a bead).* Repeat from * to * four more times. Step up. These beads form the corners.

Row 3: Peyote around with B. Step up at the end of the row. Pull the thread tight so the piece begins to form a cup.

Row 4: Add 2 A at each corner.

Note: On subsequent repeats of this row, peyote between the corners with B. Step up.

Row 5: Peyote around with B but add 1 A between the 2 A beads at each corner. Step up.

Rows 6-14: Repeat rows 3-5 three more times. There'll be a single A bead at each corner and 4 B beads sticking up on each side between the corner A beads. Weave in the thread and trim.

Second Half

Work through row 14 as for the first half but don't knot or cut the thread.

Row 15: Peyote around with drop beads. These beads are the connector beads.

Join the Two Halves

Align the corners and weave back and forth between the two halves around the bead, zipping the two edges together (see page 16). Weave in the thread and trim.

SUPPLIES

Basic Beading Kit
    (see page 14)

Size 11° cylinder beads:
    color A, 1 g
    color B, 2 g

25 size 8/0 Czech drops

Deca Bead Earring

53

Deca Bead Necklace

Diamond Bead

This Diamond Bead is 1½ inches (3.8 cm) in length but may be made smaller or larger.

A Diamond Bead has two layers with four increases around the center. The north and south corners are worked with the triangle increase and the east and west corners are worked with the hexagon increase. Make the top layer of the diamond with one more row of beads than the bottom layer, then zip the two layers together along the outer edge. You may stitch in the ditch (see page 16) with size 15° beads along the outside edge. If you want to keep the bead puffed up, tweak it to the desired shape and dip it in acrylic floor polish or stuff it with yarn before zipping the edges together. Instructions are for a 1½-inch (3.8 cm) bead.

First Layer

With 2 yd (1.8 m) of thread in the needle, bring the ends together, wax well, knot, clip the tail, and melt the ends slightly.

Row 1: Pick up 4 A and form a ring secured with a lark's head knot (see page 15). Pass back through the last bead strung.

Row 2: *Add 2 A and pass through the next A.* Repeat from * to * three more times. Step up.

Row 3: *Add 2 A and pass through the next A (don't skip a bead). Peyote 1 with B, add 1 A and pass through the next A (don't skip a bead). Peyote 1 with B.* Repeat from * to * once. Step up. The corners with 2 A will be the north and south corners and the sides with 1 A will be the east and west corners.

Row 4: Add 2 A and pass through the next A at the north and south corners (don't skip a bead). Peyote the sides with B, passing through the A at the east and west corners. Step up.

Row 5: Add 2 A and pass through the next A at the north and south corners (don't skip a bead). Peyote the sides with B, adding 2 A (above the A) at the east and west corners and passing through the next B. Step up.

Row 6: Add 2 A and pass through the next A at the north and south corners (don't skip a bead). Peyote the sides with B, adding 1 A at the east and west corners and passing through the next A (don't skip a bead). Step up.

For a small bead, work rows 1-6, then repeat rows 4-6 once. On the last row of the repeat, add only 1 A at the north and south corners.

For a medium bead, work rows 1-6, then repeat rows 4-6 twice. On the last row of the repeat, add only 1 A at the north and south corners.

For a large bead, work rows 1-6, then repeat rows 4-6 three more times. On the last row of the repeat, add only 1 A at the north and south corners.

Sew a nailhead to the center of the diamond. Add a faux bezel around the

SUPPLIES

**Basic Beading Kit
    (see page 14)**

**Size 11° cylinder beads:
    color A, 4 g (these form the
    spokes of the diamond)
    color B, 4 g**

**Size 15° round seed beads, char-
lottes, or 3-cuts, 1 g**

**2 nailheads (flat-back beads),
6 mm**

nailhead (see page 17) using the size 15° beads. Weave in the thread and trim.

Second Layer

Make the second layer the same as the first layer but don't work the last row. Sew on a nailhead and add a faux bezel.

Join the Two Layers

Weave through the beads so the thread exits the single bead at the tip of the north corner of the first layer. Align the corners and weave back and forth between the two layers around the bead, zipping the two edges together (see page 16). Weave in the thread and trim.

Add an Edge Accent

With the thread exiting a corner bead, stitch in the ditch (see page 16) with size 15° seed beads along the outside edge.

ART DECO
INSPIRATIONS

TRIANGLE BEZEL

Inspired by the geometric shapes of Art Deco architecture, illustration, and jewelry, this sparkling pendant looks as modern today as it would have in the 1920s. The bezel is a triangle with pointed corners and an open back.

Reverse side of Triangle Bezel with Swarovski volcano triangle crystal

▶ With 3 yd (2.7 m) of thread in the needle, bring the ends together, wax well, knot, clip the tail, and melt the ends slightly.

Row 1: Pick up 1 A and 11 B three times and form a ring secured with a lark's head knot (see page 15). Pass back through the last bead strung. Orient the work so you're working counter-clockwise (lefties, work clockwise).

Row 2: Peyote around with B, adding 2 A above the A bead at each corner. Step up. **Note:** The step-up will move diagonally to the left. You'll have 5 B sticking up between the corners on each side of the triangle.

Rows 3-6: Peyote around with B; when you exit an A at each corner, add 2 A and pass through the next A. After completing row 6, there'll be 9 B sticking up on each side between the corners and 5 pairs of increase A beads at each corner. Step up.

Row 7: Peyote around with B; when you exit an A at each corner, add only 1 A and pass through the next A. Step up.

(continued on next page)

Left: Triangle Bezel with Swarovski volcano triangle crystal strung with 3-mm round beads and cylinder beads

Far Left: Triangle Bezel with heliotrope triangle crystal strung with 3-mm round beads and cylinder beads

SUPPLIES

Basic Beading Kit (see page 14)

Size 11° cylinder beads:

color A, 1 g

color B, 3 g

Triangular glass stone, 23 mm (Swarovski #4727)

**Triangle Bezel made
with vintage buttons**

Reverse side

Row 8: Peyote around with B. Step up.

Row 9: Peyote around with B, adding 1 A above the A at each corner. Step up. Pull the thread tight so the piece begins to form a cup.

Row 10: Peyote around with B. There'll be an up bead on each side of each corner. Step up.

Row 11: Keeping the tension tight, peyote around with B; when you exit the last B before a corner, decrease by passing through the next B that's sticking up just past the corner (don't add a bead). Step up. Insert the glass stone.

Row 12: Keeping the tension tight, peyote around with B; when you exit the last B before a corner, decrease by passing through the next B that's sticking up just past the corner (don't add a bead). Step up. *Note:* This row may be worked with a contrasting color to frame the cabochon.

Row 13: To reinforce the bezel, pass the thread through all the beads of the last two rows (both up and down beads). At each corner, after exiting the last B, decrease by passing through the next B that's sticking up just past the corner. (Don't add a bead at the corners.) Reinforce the corners by passing through these corner beads again in a circular fashion. Weave in the thread and trim.

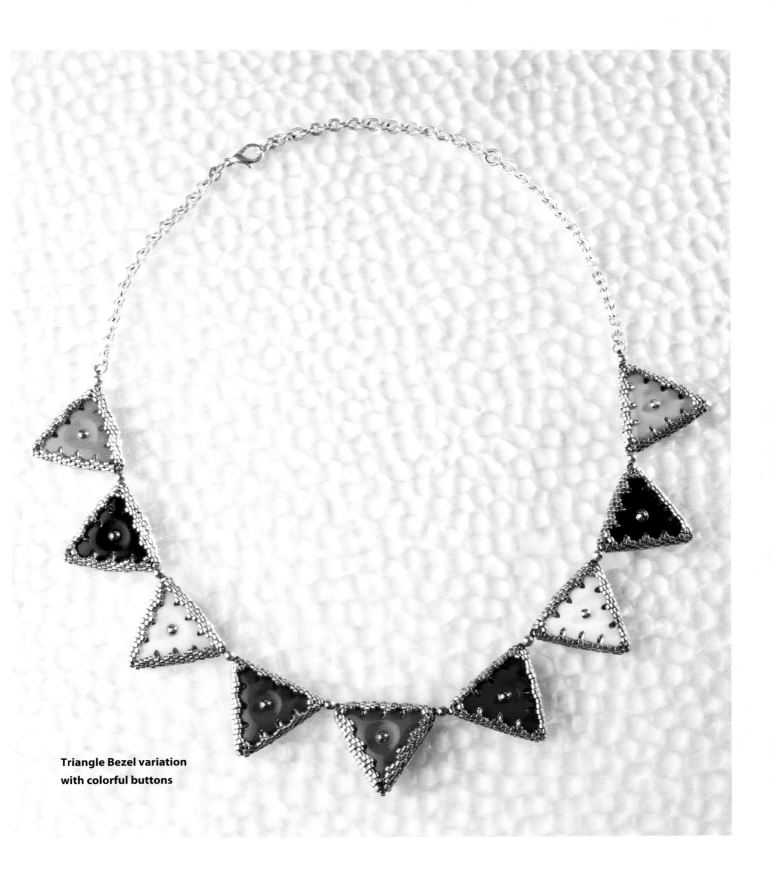

**Triangle Bezel variation
with colorful buttons**

JEWELED NECKLACE

This necklace is typical of many in the Art Deco style, both in its use of geometric shapes and its color scheme of sapphire and silver. Featuring a series of square cabochons accented with a single round cabochon in the center, it looks authentic enough to be mistaken for an antique.

▶ **Square Pendants (make 14)**

Rows 1-7: Work the first 7 rows of the Basic Square (see page 21).

Row 8: Add only 2 B beads at each corner instead of 3.

Row 9: Work 1 row of peyote. Don't cut the thread.

Glue the square cabochon to the beadwork and allow it to dry.

Row 10: Work circular peyote adding only 1 B bead at each corner.

Pass through the last two rows of beads a second time to tighten. Weave in the thread and trim.

▶ **Round Center Pendant (make 1)**

Rows 1-5: Work the first 5 rows of the Basic Hexagon (see page 24).

Rows 6-8: Repeat rows 3-5 once. Don't cut the thread.

Glue the round cabochon to the beadwork and allow it to dry.

(continued on next page)

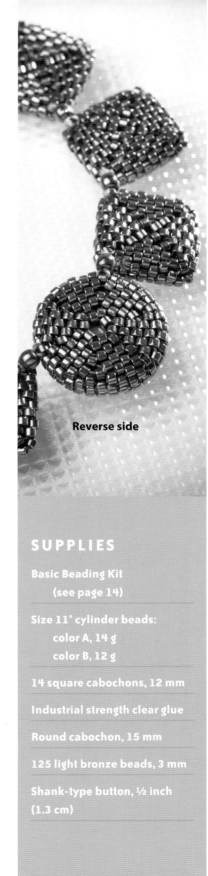

Reverse side

63

SUPPLIES

**Basic Beading Kit
(see page 14)**

**Size 11° cylinder beads:
color A, 14 g
color B, 12 g**

14 square cabochons, 12 mm

Industrial strength clear glue

Round cabochon, 15 mm

125 light bronze beads, 3 mm

**Shank-type button, ½ inch
(1.3 cm)**

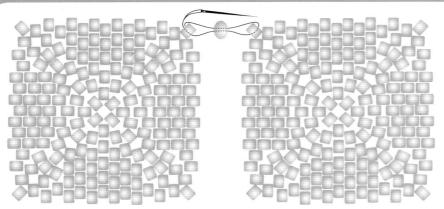

Rows 9-13: Work circular peyote, adjusting the number of rows as necessary depending on the height of the cabochon. Pass through the last two rows once more to tighten. Weave in the thread and trim.

▶ Join the Square Pendants

Join the corner bead of one square to the corner bead of another square with a 3-mm round bead between. Sew back and forth in a figure-eight pattern as shown in figure 1. Join seven squares for one side of the necklace and seven squares for the other side.

▶ Connect the Round Center Pendant

Connect the corner bead of the last square on one side of the necklace to a corner bead in the round shape. Connect the corner bead of the next square on the other side of the necklace to the round shape, skipping a corner bead in the base of the round shape (figure 2).

▶ Make the Netted Chain

Row 1: With thread anchored and exiting a corner bead of the top square on one side of the necklace, string one 3-mm bead and 3 B 17 times. Add enough B beads to make a loop for the button. Pass back through the last 3-mm bead.

Row 2: *Add 3 B, one 3-mm round bead, and 3 B and pass through the second 3-mm counting from where your thread exits a 3-mm bead.* Repeat from * to * along the row. When you exit the second-to-last 3-mm bead, add 3 B and one 3-mm bead and pass through the middle bead in the side of the square cabochon, then back through the 3-mm bead.

Row 3: Repeat row 2. When you come to the second-to-last 3-mm bead, pass through it, the next 3 B, the 2-mm and the loop of beads. Then continue through the 3-mm at the base of the loop.

Row 4: Repeat row 2. When exiting the last 3-mm bead, add 3 B and one 3-mm, pass through the corner bead of the square and back through the 3-mm bead. Weave in the thread and trim.

Work the netted chain for the other side the same way, except instead of adding a loop of beads for the button, add 3 B, the button shank, and 3 B.

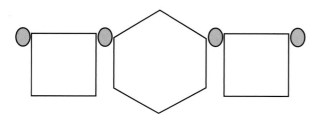

ELEGANCE

Window shoppers strolling along the Champs Élysées in Paris during the 1920s may very well have admired a necklace similar to this one, glimmering on display. Silver and black beads couple with the smooth surface of black onyx to give this necklace a simple yet sophisticated style with the sleek elegance of Art Deco jewelry.

▶ Work the Elongated (Isosceles) Triangle (see page 29) for 12 rows, adding a single A at each corner on the last row. Stitch in the ditch (see page 16) along the increase lines with rose montées. Sew the drop bead to the narrow tip of the triangle adding a single cylinder bead below it and passing back through the drop bead. Weave in the thread and trim.

▶ With 1½ yd (1.4 m) of thread in the needle, bring the ends together, wax well, knot, clip the tail, and melt slightly. Attach one half of the clasp to the thread with a lark's head knot (see page 15). String beads, alternating 3-mm round beads with cut cylinder beads to desired length. Pass through the corner bead of the triangle, then back through the strand of beads, around the clasp, and back through the last bead. Knot between the beads, weave in the tail, and trim. Repeat for the other side. Glue the triangle to the donut.

Reverse side

CHAPTER SIX

ETHNIC
INSPIRATIONS

CELTIC TREFOIL

Perhaps the oldest use of the trefoil as a symbol was discovered in ancient Egypt on the royal couch of Tutankhamen. There it was a stylized geometric representation of three sun disks fused together to represent the unity of the gods of the sun, water and earth. Later in ancient Ireland, it represented the three-leafed shamrock, a sacred plant among the Celtic Druids. Legend has it that St. Patrick himself plucked a shamrock from the grass to illustrate the doctrine of the Christian trinity. Wear this beaded version and who knows, perhaps the road will rise to meet you and the wind will always be at your back!

SUPPLIES

Basic Beading Kit (see page 14)

Size 11° cylinder beads:
    color A, 1 g
    color B-1* (edge accent), 3 g
    color B-2* (main color), 4 g

Size 11° cut or round seed beads, 2 g

120 round beads, 3 mm (optional)

Necklace clasp (optional)

Tassel (optional)

Industrial strength clear glue (optional)

Pin back, 1 inch (2.5 cm) (optional)

* Note: Make sure there's good contrast between the B-1 and B-2 beads. Place them side by side on a needle to check. Non-matte beads work best.

69

I recommend you work a Pointed Oval Link (see page 92) before beginning this project.

▶ First Layer

With 2 yd (1.8 m) of thread in the needle, bring the ends together, wax well, knot, clip the tail, and melt the ends slightly.

Row 1: Use edge accent (B-1) beads for this row. Pick up 1 A, 29 B-1, 4 A, 29 B-1, 4 A, 29 B-1 and 3 A. Slide the beads to within 1 inch (2.5 cm) of the knot. Carefully tie the strand of beads into an overhand knot as shown in figure 1 (page 70). Separate the strands between the beads and the knot at the end of the thread. Pass the needle between the two strands to form a ring secured with a lark's head knot (see page 15). Slide the beads toward the knot to close the gap. Pass back through the

last bead strung. Don't let the knot slip inside a bead. Orient the work so you're working counter-clockwise (lefties, work clockwise). Hold the work between your thumb and forefinger to keep it flat and work with medium tension. **Note:** Be careful not to let the beads twist as you work the next row of peyote.

Row 2: Use B-2 beads for rows 2-6. *Add 2 A and pass through the next A, peyote 16 with B-2.* Repeat from * to * two more times. Be sure this row isn't twisted before stepping up through the first A added. The beads will be in a twisted pretzel-like form, but the Celtic knot pattern will be obvious after the next row.

Rows 3-6: Add 2 A at each corner and peyote the sides with B-2. Make certain to add a B-2 before you pass through the first up B bead after each corner and step up at the end of each row. Keep the rows flat. When row 6 is completed, there'll be 7 pairs of A beads at each corner.

Row 7: Use edge accent (B-1) beads for this row. Add 1 A at each corner and peyote the sides with B-1.

▶ **Second Layer**

After stepping up, pass through the column of A beads on the left at the same corner, toward the beginning row. End so the thread exits the last A bead, a down bead (figure 2).

Row 2: Work row 2 as for the first layer but with B-1 (edge accent) beads. Push these beads toward the outer edge of the trefoil. ***Note:*** The step-up for each row will move to the left on this layer.

Rows 3-7: Work 5 rows with B-2 beads as in the first layer. On the last row, don't work past the step up.

Zip the second layer to the first layer along the outer edge (see page 16). At the corners, pass through the first A bead on the right of the second layer, then through the single bead at the tip of the first layer, then through the A bead on the left of the second layer and continue to zip around. Stitch the layers together where they intersect. Weave in the thread and trim. ***Optional:*** Stitch in the ditch (see page 16) with round or cut size 11° seed beads along the outer edge.

Add a tassel if desired. To make a necklace, string beads with a clasp as described in Adding a Strand of Beads (page 15). To make a pendant, glue or stitch a pin back to the back of the beadwork.

70

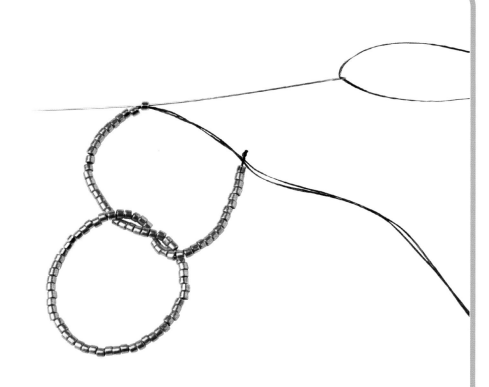

figure 1

Tie the strand of beads with an overhand knot, secure with a lark's head knot, and pass back through the last bead.

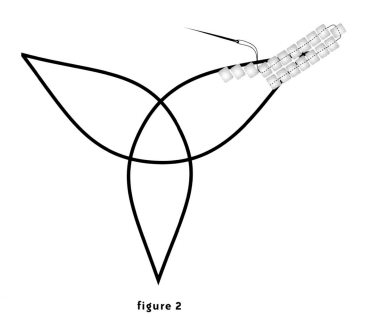

figure 2

SUPPLIES

Basic Beading Kit (see page 14)

Size 11° cylinder beads:
    silver-lined blue matte, 2 g
    pumpkin, 2 g

Size 11° round silver seed beads, 2 g

Size 15° silver seed beads

2 earring findings

2 sew-on turquoise cabochons or nailheads (flat-backed beads), 6 mm

Reverse side

BERBER EARRINGS

The Berber people form a major section of the population of Libya, Algeria, and Morocco. Typical Berber vestments often include colorful jewelry of silver enameled with deep blue and pumpkin yellow, with accents of carnelian and turquoise. Transport yourself to Northern Africa with these drop earrings that mimic this style.

▶ Blue Teardrop

Rows 1-10: Use blue cylinder beads and follow instructions for the Teardrop (see page 27). On row 10, add 6 beads at the tip instead of 2, forming a loop to suspend the dangle from the earring finding.

Row 11: Peyote around with size 11° silver seed beads. Weave in the thread and trim. Repeat for second teardrop.

▶ Yellow Triangle

Rows 1-5: With ¾ yd (.69 m) of single yellow thread, work rows 1-5 of the Basic Triangle (see page 20).

Row 6: Work as for Basic Triangle but add 4 beads at each corner instead of 2.

Row 7: Peyote the sides with silver seed beads but don't add beads at the corners.

Sew the cabochon or nailhead to the center of the triangle. Add a faux bezel (see page 17) around the cabochon with size 15° silver seed beads. Weave in the thread and trim. Repeat for second triangle.

▶ Assemble the Earrings

Sew the triangle to the blue drop shape. Attach the earring finding to the loop at the top of the drop. Repeat for the second earring.

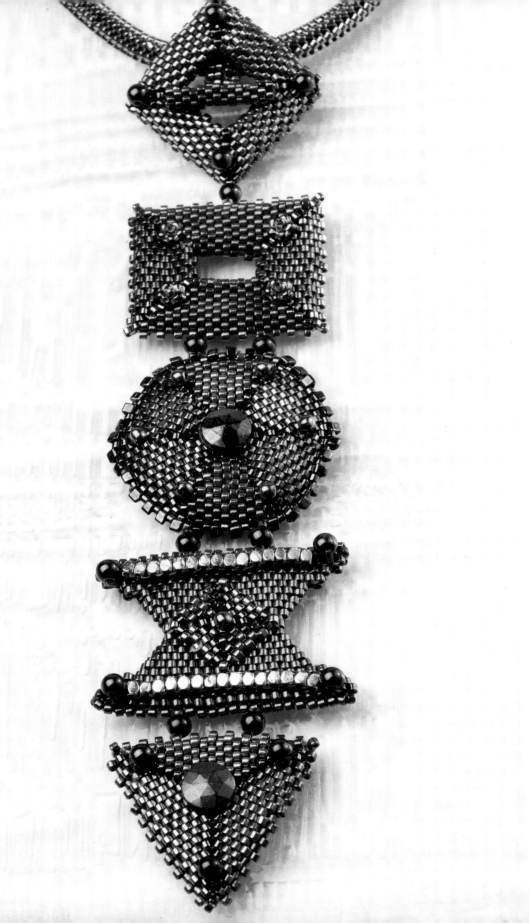

TUAREG PENDANT

This beaded pendant was inspired by metal pendants worn by wealthy Niger Tuareg men and women in Mali. The pendants, used as counterweights to hold head cloths in place and known as *assrou n' swoul*, fasten to a corner of the fabric and hang down the back. These elaborate key-like pendants are highly valued pieces made of iron, silver, copper, and brass. The round copper beads used in this beaded pendant represent the copper spheres used to accent the elements in a Tuareg pendant.

Reverse side

▶ The Chain

Work six-bead tubular herringbone chain (see page 114) with dark silver beads around the satin cord for 17 inches (43.2 cm) or desired length. Wrap the cord ends with thread and sew the ends of the herringbone tube to the cord. Anchor the thread in the cord and add a bead cap, a 4-mm copper bead, and one side of the silver clasp. Stitch back and forth until the toggle is securely attached. Weave in the thread tail and trim. Repeat for the other end.

▶ The Toggle

A toggle attached to the center front of the chain is used to suspend the pendant from the chain. The toggle bar passes through the open square so the pendant is removable. Toggle instructions are given on page 17. Attach it to the chain with two loops of single-needle ladder stitch.

(continued on next page)

SUPPLIES

Basic Beading Kit (see page 14)

Size 11° cylinder beads:
  dark silver, 12 g
  silver, 10 g
  copper, 10 g

20 inches (50.8 cm) black satin cord, 2 mm

2 silver bead caps, 5 mm

16 round copper beads, 4 mm

Silver clasp

4 flat daisy rondelles, 4 mm

2 copper nailheads (flat-back beads), 8 mm

7 round copper beads, 3 mm

30 silver cube beads, 3 mm

▶ Open Square Element

Follow the instructions for the Open Square on page 34 as follows.

Pick up 1 dark silver and 9 silver cylinder beads four times for row 1. Use silver for the sides of the square and dark silver for the increases at the corners. Work the last 2 rows with copper. Sew a 4-mm copper bead to each corner. Weave in the thread and trim.

▶ Open Rectangle Element

Work the element with copper and the corner increases with dark silver.

Row 1: Follow the instructions for the Rectangle on page 34 but use 1 dark silver, 9 copper, 1 dark silver, and 5 copper cylinder beads twice for the beginning row.

Rows 2-11: Work rows 2-6 twice. Work the last row with silver. Work the second side with the same colors. Zip the outer edges of both rectangles together (see page 16). Stitch in the ditch with silver around the outer edge (see page 16).

Sew a 4-mm flat daisy rondelle to each corner. Weave in the thread and trim.

▶ Hexagon Element

Rows 1-8: Follow directions for the Basic Hexagon, rows 1-8 (see page 24), using dark silver for A and silver for B.

Rows 9-14: Repeat rows 6-8 two times.

Rows 15-20: Repeat rows 6-8 two times with dark silver for A, but using copper for B.

Sew one 8-mm nailhead to the center and a 3-mm round copper bead at each increase near the edge.

Work the back side like the front side, but work one less row.

Align the two pieces and zip them together along the edge (page 16). Stitch in the ditch with copper along the outer edge. Weave in the thread and trim.

▶ Hourglass Element

This element is worked with brick stitch (see page 113). Make two identical pieces for the front and back and stitch them together along the edges. Working with copper, begin in the middle and work toward the top, then stitch back to the middle and work toward the bottom.

Row 1: Single-needle ladder 3 beads tall and 11 beads long.

Rows 2-6: 1 bead tall. Increase at the end of the row.

Rows 7-8: 1 bead tall. Increase 2 beads on both ends of the row.

Row 9: 1 bead tall. Increase at the end of the row.

Work 2 single-needle ladders with 3-mm silver cubes. Make each ladder 1 bead tall and 15 beads long. Sew one of the cube ladders centered and one bead below the top edge and parallel to it. Sew the second ladder centered and one bead up from the bottom edge and parallel to it. Sew a 4-mm round copper bead at each end of the cube ladders. Weave in the thread and trim.

▶ Square Embellishment for the Center of the Hourglass

Use dark silver for A and silver for B.

Rows 1-4: Work rows 1-4 of the Basic Square (see page 21).

Row 5: Work row 6 of the Basic Square.

Sew this square on point to the center front of the hourglass shape, adding a 3-mm round copper bead at the center.

Work the back side like the front side but without the embellishments. Align the two hourglass shapes one on top of the other and join the side and bottom edges with a whipstitch or overcast stitch, adding one bead with each stitch. Weave in the thread and trim.

▶ Triangle Element

Make a two-sided triangle as outlined below.

First layer: Work the first 10 rows using dark silver for A and silver for B.

Rows 1-4: Work rows 1-4 of the Basic Triangle (see page 20).

Rows 5-10: Repeat row 4.

Row 11: Repeat row 4 using copper beads.

Sew one 4-mm round copper bead at each corner of the triangle and an 8-mm copper nailhead to the center.

Work the second triangle like the first triangle but work one extra row, row 12, with copper, adding only 1 bead at each corner.

Align the two triangles and zip them together. Stitch in the ditch with copper along the outer edge. Weave in the thread and trim.

▶ Join the Elements

Join each element to the next one using one or two 4-mm round copper beads as follows: With thread anchored and exiting a bead in the appropriate place, add the 4-mm bead and pass through a bead in the next element, then back through the 4-mm bead and into the bead your thread originally exited, but from the other side. The thread will make a figure-eight pattern. Stitch in this pattern twice. Weave in the thread and trim.

CROSS OF AGADEZ

The city of Agadez is an ancient crossroads for camel caravans crossing the Sahara. The Tuareg, a nomadic people who once traveled the desert, wore crossed-shaped pendants of different designs to identify their birthplace. The ornaments would pass from father to son with the solemn words, "My son, I give you the four corners of the world, because one cannot know where one will die." Made of silver, the crosses were sometimes used as currency to buy cattle, cloth, or food. In the modern world, you won't be able to trade this necklace for a plane ticket, but you can certainly wear it as you travel the four corners of the map.

Reverse side

▶ **Squares (make 3)**

Rows 1-11: Work rows 1-11 of the Basic Square (see page 21) with cylinder beads.

Rows 12-15: Repeat rows 7-11.

Rows 16-18: Repeat rows 7-9. On the last row don't add the 2 beads at the corners, just pass through the 3 beads added in the previous row.

Glue a cabochon to the center of the square and add a faux bezel of 15° seed beads (see page 17). Sew a 4-mm daisy rondelle held in place with a 2-mm round silver bead between the cabochon and each corner.

Work the back of the pendant like the front, but end with row 17. Align the front and back pieces and join by zipping the edges together (see page 16). Sew a 5-mm rondelle and 2-mm round bead on the outer edge at each of three corners. Weave in the thread and trim.

(continued on next page)

SUPPLIES

Basic Beading Kit (see page 14)

Size 11° nickel-plated cylinder beads, 16 g

Industrial strength clear glue

3 oval cabochons, 9 x 13 mm

Size 15° seed beads, 1 g

12 Bali silver daisy rondelles, 4 mm

28 round silver beads, 2 mm

12 Bali silver daisy rondelles, 5 mm

Plastic-coated beading wire, 22 inches (55.9 cm)

2 crimp beads

Clasp

32 Bali silver daisy rondelles, 6 mm

10 oval green beads, approximately 10 x 16 mm

12 round green beads, 8 mm

6 round bone beads, 10 mm

2 crimp beads

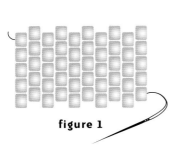

figure 1

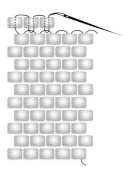

figure 2

figure 3

▶ **Tube Beads**

Work a piece of flat peyote with cylinder beads 10 beads wide and 10 rows long (figure 1). Add 1 row of brick stitch (5 beads) along one side edge (figure 2). Fold to form a tube and zip the edges together (see page 16).

▶ **Embellish the Tube**

Pass through one bead on the edge. Add a cylinder bead and, skipping a bead in the tube, pass through the next bead (figure 3). Continue across the row. At the end of the row, turn and pass through the next bead on the edge. Work another row in the opposite direction. Continue back

and forth until you have completed five rows. Center the pendant on a corner of the tube and sew the tube and pendant together with a 5-mm rondelle between them. Don't stitch all the way through the tube as it'll make it difficult to string later. Weave in the thread and trim.

▶ **Assemble the Necklace**

Use beading wire and pick up 1 crimp bead and one side of the clasp, then pass back through the crimp bead and flatten it. *Add one 6-mm rondelle, 1 oval green bead, one 6-mm rondelle and 1 round green bead.* Repeat from * to * four more times. *Add one 6-mm rondelle, 1 bone bead, one 6-mm rondelle, 1 pendant, one 6-mm rondelle, 1 bone bead, one 6-mm rondelle and 1 round green bead.* Repeat from * to * two more times. Add remaining beads for the rest of the strand to mirror the first side. Add 1 crimp bead and the other side of the clasp, pass back through the crimp bead and flatten it.

SUPPLIES

Basic Beading Kit (see page 14)

Size 11° cylinder beads:
    color A, 4 g
    color B, 8 g

Cabochon or nailhead (flat-back bead), 12 mm

Industrial strength clear glue (optional, if cabochon is used)

Size 15° seed beads, 1 g

8 bugle beads, 12 mm

4 round black beads, 2 mm

4 bead caps, 8 mm

4 seed beads, size 11°

4 round beads, 3 mm

Closed ring or split ring, 6 mm

22 to 24 inches (55.9 to 61 cm) of chain

Acrylic floor polish

NORTH STAR

The North Star, also known as Polaris, sits at the end of the Little Dipper's handle. From ancient times mariners used it to guide their navigation; here, the popular star shows the way by serving as inspiration for a pendant. Its silver and black beads give it the look of an amulet belonging to the distant past.

Reverse side

▶ Square Center

Rows 1-11: Work rows 1-11 of the Basic Square (see page 21).

▶ Star Points (make 4)

Rows 1-8: Work rows 1-8 of the Elongated (Isosceles) Triangle (see page 25).

Row 9: Work as for row 9 of the Isosceles Triangle but add only 1 bead at each corner.

▶ Assembly

Zip one triangle to each side of the square

(see page 16). Glue the cabochon or sew the nailhead to the center and add a faux bezel of 15° seed beads (see page 17). Sew bugle beads with a 2-mm round black bead between each along the outer edges of the square. Center bead caps on the triangles and sew in place with size 11° black seed beads. Add one row of B around the entire outer edge of the star, then add a 3-mm round bead at each corner and attach the ring to one of the tips. Weave in the thread and trim. Apply acrylic floor polish to stiffen the pendant.

MINARET BEAD

The melodious call to prayer rings out from the minaret, the distinctive tower that rise from a mosque. Usually taller than the surrounding buildings, these spires can featur all sorts of architectural flourishes, including onion-shaped domes, pointed roof arcades, and crenellation. The minaret is interpreted in miniature in this bead, whic can stand alone as a pendant or be combined with other shape

Rows 1-5: Work rows 1-5.

Rows 6-14: Work rows 3-5 three times, but work row 14 with A. There'll be four up beads between the corner beads. Sew on nailheads and add faux bezels with size 15° seed beads (see page 17). Weave through the beads so the thread exits the top center of the piece and add the bead cap, a 2-mm bead, and the closed ring, pass back through the 2-mm bead and the bead cap, and stitch through a bead in the beginning ring. Weave in the thread and trim.

Rows 15-25: Anchor a new thread in the last row so it exits an up bead just past a corner. Continue working in even-count peyote with a step-up at the end of each row for 11 rows without increasing. To keep track of the corners, continue to place an A below the corner beads every other row. Sew nailheads to the tube and add faux bezels if desired.

Rows 26-28: Pass back to the last increase row (row 14 worked with A) and, stitching in the ditch (see page 16), work rows 3-5 of the Pouff. These rows extend from the domed top and overhang the tubular section.
Optional: Work the last row with size 11° seed beads with a 2-mm bead at each corner.

Rows 29-30: Decrease at each corner by skipping from the up B to the next up B. Pinch the sides together to shape the bead work.

Rows 31-32: Work even-count peyote stitc for 8 rows with B, continuing to place A every other row to indicate the corners and stepping up at the end of each row.

Rows 33-38: *Peyote around with B, decrea ing at each corner. Then work two even rov of peyote.* Repeat from * to * once. End with 5 beads in the ring. Pass through the 5 beads twice to tighten.

Add the second bead cap, the 6-mm bead and seven strands of fringe using size 15° seed beads with a 1-mm bead or size 11° seed bead at the end of each strand. Each strand should be 15 to 20 beads long. Pass back through the size 15° seed beads, the 6-mm bead, and the bead cap, then pass through a bead in the final ring. When the 6-mm bead is filled with thread and it isn't possible to pass your needle through, make a half-hitch knot around the strands of frinc between the fringe and the 6-mm bead, an then add remaining strands of fringe. Pass through the 6-mm bead and the bead cap and into the beadwork. Weave in the threac and trim.

SUPPLIES

Basic Beading Kit (see page 14)

Size 11° cylinder beads:
    color A, 3 g
    color B, 5 g

10 round nailheads (flat-back beads), 5 mm

Size 15° seed beads, 3-cut or round, 2 g

2 bead caps, 8 mm

7 round beads, 2 mm

Closed ring, 6 mm

Size 11° seed beads, 1 g

Any shape bead, 6 to 8 mm

7 round beads, 1 mm or size 11° seed beads for fringe ends

POUFF BEAD

Imagine yourself in a Marrakesh café, sipping mint tea and lounging on an array of pouffs—Moroccan cushions made of leather, frequently patterned with elaborate silk embroidery. Inspired by this furnishing, the Pouff Bead is embellished with nailheads, faux bezels, and bead caps.

▶ First Half

Begin with 2 yd (1.8 m) of thread, bring the ends together, wax well, knot, clip the tail and melt the ends slightly. Follow the instructions for the Deca Bead (page 53) as follows:

Rows 1-5: Work rows 1-5.

Rows 6-17: Repeat rows 3-5 four more times.

The last row is the connector bead row. There'll be 5 B sticking up on each side and 1 A at each corner. **Optional:** On this row, substitute a 1- or 2-mm round bead for the A at each corner and use size 11° seed beads in place of the B on the sides.

Pass back to the beginning ring and sew on the bead cap with a size 11° seed bead. Sew a nailhead or glue a cabochon in each of the five sections and add a faux bezel with size 15° seed beads (see page 17) around each one. Weave in the thread and trim.

▶ Second Half

Rows 1-16: Work like the first half but don't add row 17 and don't trim the thread.

Align the corners and zip the first and second halves together (see page 16). Sew a 2-mm bead and the closed ring to one of the corners. Weave in the thread and trim. Dip in acrylic floor polish and allow to dry.

SUPPLIES

Basic Beading Kit (see page 14)

Size 11° cylinder beads:

    color A, 2 g

    color B, 2 g

5 round beads, 2 or 3 mm

Size 11° seed beads, 1 g

2 bead caps, 8 mm

10 nailheads (flat-back beads) or cabochons, 3 to 5 mm

Industrial strength clear glue (optional, if cabochons are used)

Size 15° seed beads, 1 g

Closed ring, 6 mm

Acrylic floor polish

CHANDELIER BEAD

This beaded version of a typical chandelier dangle is embellished with nailheads and faux bezels.

▶ Sides (make 4)

Rows 1-6: Work rows 1-6 of the Elongated (Isosceles) Triangle (see page 25).

On row 6 add 2 A at the left and right corners and 4 A at the elongated lower corner. Pass thread to the beginning row and sew 1 nailhead centered over the beginning row. Add a faux bezel with size 15° seed beads (see page 17). Weave in the thread and trim.

▶ Bottom

With 2 yd (1.8 m) of thread in your needle, bring ends together, wax well, knot, clip the tail, and melt the ends slightly.

Row 1: Pick up 4 A beads and form a ring secured with a lark's head knot (see page 15). Pass back through the last bead strung.

SUPPLIES

Basic Beading Kit (see page 14)

Size 11° cylinder beads:

color A, 2 g

color B, 2 g

8 nailheads (flat-back beads),
3 to 8 mm

6 round beads, 2 mm

Size 11° seed beads, 1 g

Size 15° seed beads, 1 g

2 silver daisy rondelles, 5 mm

Closed ring, 6 mm

Row 2: Add 1 A and pass through the next A (don't skip a bead) four times. Step up.

Row 3: Add 2 A and pass through the next A at the corner four times. Step up. These pairs of A beads form a V and become a corner of the square.

Row 4: *Add 1 A between the 2 A beads that form a V in the previous row. Peyote 1 with B on each side.* Repeat from * to * three more times. Step up.

Row 5: Peyote around with B. Step up.

Row 6: Add 3 A above each A and peyote the sides with B. Step up.

Row 7: At each corner, after exiting the first A of the set of three at that corner, add 2 A and pass through the third A. Peyote the sides with B. Step up.

Row 8: Add 1 A between the 2 A beads at each corner. Peyote the sides with B. Step up.

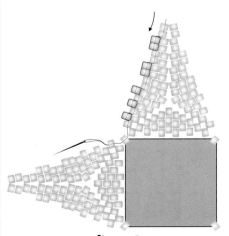

figure 1

Rows: 9-12: Repeat rows 5-8 once. (**Optional:** In the last row, substitute a 2-mm round bead or size 11° seed bead for the single A at each corner.) There'll be 5 B beads sticking up between the corner beads on each side. Sew on nailheads and add faux bezels if desired.

Zip one triangle to each side of the square (see page 16), passing through the single corner beads on the square.

Anchor the thread so it exits the two beads at the narrow tip of a triangle going toward the base. *Add 2 B and pass through 2 B twice; add 1 B and pass through the next bead three times. Pass through the single corner bead in the square, then zip the triangle edge just completed to the next triangle (figure 1). Add 1 A and pass down through the two beads at the top of the next triangle.* Repeat from * to * for the remaining three sides. Pass through the four beads added at the top of the piece.

Add a silver daisy rondelle, a 2-mm round bead and the closed ring at the top. Pass back through these beads to the opposite top bead. Repeat to reinforce, weave in the thread and trim.

TRIANGLE BEAD

The triangle may be a basic shape, but it's also one of the forms identified by Plato in formulating his solution to the problems of the universe. Not bad for a little polygon! To ancient Pythagoreans, the triangle represented the essence of stability. For this triangle bead, an extra dimension is formed with the addition of bezeled cabochons.

SUPPLIES

Basic Beading Kit (see page 14)

Size 11° cylinder beads:
    color A, 2 g
    color B, 3 g

4 cabochons or nailheads (flat-back beads), 6 to 8 mm

Industrial strength clear glue (optional, if using cabochons)

Size 15° seed beads, 1 g

Round metal bead, 2 mm

Closed ring, 6 mm

Make this bead by following the instructions for the Tetra Bead (page 46) but work each triangle with 20 rows. On row 20 add only one A bead at each corner. Glue a cabochon or sew a nailhead to each side and add a faux bezel with size 15° seed beads (see page 17). Sew a 2-mm bead and closed ring to one corner. Weave in the thread and trim.

PYRAMID BEAD

From Egypt to China, India, and Mesoamerica, pyramids have been erected as places of religious significance or as monuments to the departed. You won't need a large crew to help you construct a pyramid bead, but adding one to your jewelry may mean as much to you as erecting the Great Pyramid of Giza did to its builders.

SUPPLIES

Basic Beading Kit (see page 14)

Size 11° cylinder beads:

    color A, 2 g

    color B, 2 g

5 round beads, 2 mm

Size 11° seed beads, 1 g

Cabochon or nailhead (flat-back bead) for the bottom, 8 mm

Industrial strength clear glue (optional, if cabochon is used)

4 nailheads for the top sides, 5 mm

4 nailheads for the top side edges, 3 mm

Daisy rondelle, 5 mm

Silver bead, 6 mm

Closed ring, 6 mm

▶ Bottom

Rows 1-11: Work rows 1-11 of the Basic Square (see page 21).

Rows 12-15: Repeat rows 7-10 once.

Row 16: Repeat row 11, placing a 2-mm round bead or size 11° seed bead at each corner.

Glue a cabochon or sew a nailhead in the center. Add a faux bezel (see page 17). Weave in the thread and trim.

▶ Top

Rows 1-5: Work rows 1-5 of the Octa Bead.

Rows 6-22: Repeat rows 3-5 five times, then repeat rows 3 and 4 once. There'll be 6 up B

beads on each side. Sew a 5-mm nailhead to each side and add faux bezels. Sew a 3-mm nailhead along each increase area. Don't trim the thread.

▶ Ring

Weave through the bead so the thread exits a bead in the beginning ring. Add the daisy rondelle, a 6-mm silver bead (optional), a 2-mm round bead, and the closed ring. Pass back through all the beads and through a bead opposite where the thread exited originally. Repeat to reinforce. Pass the thread back to the last row. Align the corners of the top and bottom and zip together (see page 16). Weave in the thread and trim.

LANTERN BEAD

Moroccan lanterns are most often made of iron, copper, brass, and bronze, and you can choose a palette of beads that suggest these metals. Some lanterns have colorful inserts of blue, green, red, or amber glass; emulate this look by embellishing your bead with transparent beads to give the impression of a glowing candle within. This bead may light your path to a love of shapes, and it will certainly add sparkle to your jewelry.

▶ Top and Sides

Rows 1-5: Work rows 1-5 of the Deca Bead (see page 53).

Rows 6-11: Repeat rows 3-5 twice.

Weave through the beads so the thread exits a bead at the top center of the piece. Add the bead cap, a 2-mm bead, and the closed ring, then pass back through the 2-mm bead and the bead cap. Weave through the beads to the last row of peyote so the thread exits a down bead.

Rows 12-29: With B, work in circular peyote with a step-up at the end of each row, placing an A bead below the corner A beads in every other row.

Sew a nailhead to each section of the tube and add faux bezels with size 15° seed beads (see page 17). Weave through the beads to the last row of peyote above the tubular section (row 11) so the thread exits a corner bead. Stitch in the ditch (see page 16) around with A or B. Weave in the thread and trim.

▶ Bottom

Rows 1-8: Work rows 1-8 of the Basic Pentagon (see page 23). Weave through the beads to the beginning ring and add a bead cap and a 2-mm bead. Pass back through the bead cap into the beginning ring. Pass thread through to the last row.

Align the corners of the pentagon just completed to the bottom of the previously completed tube and zip the edges together (see page 16). Extend the edge of the pentagon by working rows 5-8 once. Weave in the thread and trim.

SUPPLIES

Basic Beading Kit (see page 14)

Size 11° cylinder beads:
    color A, 2 g
    color B, 3 g

Size 15° seed beads, 3-cut or round, 2 g

2 bead caps, 8 to 10 mm

2 round beads, 2 mm

Silver closed ring, 6 mm

5 flat round or square nailheads (flat-back beads), 5 mm

CUBE BEAD

In ancient Greece, the cube symbolized kingship and earthly foundations, and during medieval times many Gothic cathedrals were built using the geometric proportions of the cube. With its identical faces, edges, and angles, the cube has also come to represent unity. For the Cube Bead, six square sides are joined and then embellished with nailheads and faux bezels.

Follow the instructions for the Cube Bead on page 48. Embellish each side with a 5- or 6-mm nailhead and add faux bezels with size 15° seed beads (see page 17). Weave through the beads so the thread exits a corner bead. Add the daisy rondelle, a 2-mm bead, and the ring and pass back through the bead and the rondelle. Weave in the thread and trim.

SUPPLIES

Basic Beading Kit (see page 14)

Size 11° cylinder beads:

    color A, 2 g

    color B, 2 g

6 nailheads (flat-back beads), 5 or 6 mm

Size 15° seed beads, 1 g

Silver daisy rondelle, 5 mm

Silver bead, 2 mm

Closed ring, 6 mm

SEALED LOCKET

Seal a memento, a secret message, or even a tiny bell within this beaded bead, and you're participating in a tale waiting to be told. Years from now, when the thread disintegrates, someone may find your secret message and try to understand what it means.

This locket has a 9 x 13-mm cameo added to the front and is worked with one additional repeat of rows 6-8 of the Basic Oval.

▶ Front and Back

With 2 yd (1.8 m) of thread in the needle, bring the ends together, wax well, knot, clip the tail, and melt the ends slightly.

Rows 1-8: Work rows 1-8 of the Oval (see page 26).

Rows 9-11: Repeat Rows 6-8 once.

Sew a flat oval bead or nailhead in the center or glue on a cabochon. Add a faux bezel with size 15° seed beads. Sew 1 daisy rondelle to the center of each increase, anchoring the rondelle with a size 15° seed bead. Weave in the thread and trim.

Repeat for the back of the bead.

▶ Sides

Continuing off the back of the bead, work even-count peyote for 5 rows with a step-up at the end of each row but without increases to form the side of the bead. Zip the front to the side aligning the corners (see on page 16). Don't trim the thread.

▶ Add the Hanging Ring

Weave through the beads so the thread exits the top center of the oval side. Add the 8-mm bead and the closed ring, then pass back through the 8-mm bead and through a bead in the top of the oval side. Repeat once to reinforce it. Weave in the thread and trim.
Optional: To stiffen, dip the bead in acrylic floor polish and allow it to dry.

Sealed Locket Bead attached to chain links with eyepins

SUPPLIES

Basic Beading Kit (see page 14)

Size 11° cylinder beads:
    color A, 2 g
    color B, 4 g

2 flat oval beads, nailheads (flat-back beads) or cabochons, 5 x 10 mm

Industrial strength clear glue (optional, if using cabochon)

Size 15° seed beads, 3-cut or round, 1 g

12 daisy rondelles, 5 mm

Round bead, 8 mm

Closed ring, 6 mm

Acrylic floor polish

Moroccan Beads embellished with Bali silver bead caps, rondelles, and sew-on cabochons or nailheads

Left: A variation of the Moroccan Necklace made with copper cylinder beads and green nail-heads.
Below: A version of the Pouff Bead strung through the center.

MOROCCAN LANTERNS NECKLACE

Use the beaded pendants described on the previous pages to create a necklace that echoes the rich metalwork traditions of Morocco. Black nailheads offer high contrast against silver, emphasizing the geometry of the beads, but you might use silver nail-heads with copper beads for a more authentic look. The tassels are reminiscent of the elaborate gear desert nomads use to decorate their camels.

SUPPLIES

5 or more pendants

6 tassels

Satin (rattail) cord, about 1½ yd (1.4 m)

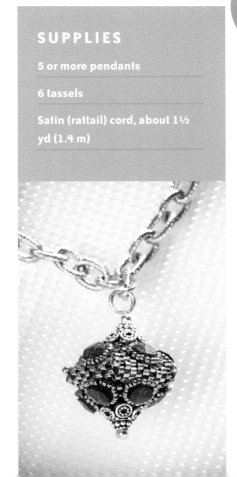

▶ Make the Beads

Make any combination of the Minaret, Pouff, Chandelier, Triangle, Pyramid, Lantern, Cube, and Sealed Locket beads described on the previous pages, adding purchased tassels.

▶ Attaching Pendants and Tassels to the Cord

String the main pendant on the satin cord and tie the cord around the pendant ring with an overhand knot. Add a tassel 1 inch (2.5 cm) from the first pendant and tie the cord around it with an overhand knot. Repeat for the remaining pendants and tassels.

▶ Finishing the Cord Ends

Make a Tube Bead (see page 78) for each of the ends of the cord. Before folding the edges to form a tube, insert the satin cord, then zip the edges together and add the extra beads on the outside. Stitch the bead to the cord and sew a tassel to the end of the tube bead.

CHAPTER SEVEN

CONTEMPORARY
INSPIRATIONS

POINTED OVAL LINKS

This simple but classic oval shape has astonishing versatility. Link the ovals together for a full but flexible chain. Attach them end-to-end with one or more beads in between for a more slinky look. Hang them from ear wires. Use them as petals for a flower. You can make the links larger or smaller by increasing or decreasing the number of B beads in the first row by two and increasing or decreasing the number of peyote stitches in subsequent rows.

SUPPLIES

Basic Beading Kit (see page 14)

Size 11° cylinder beads:
    color A, 6 g
    color B, 27 g
    color C, 8 g

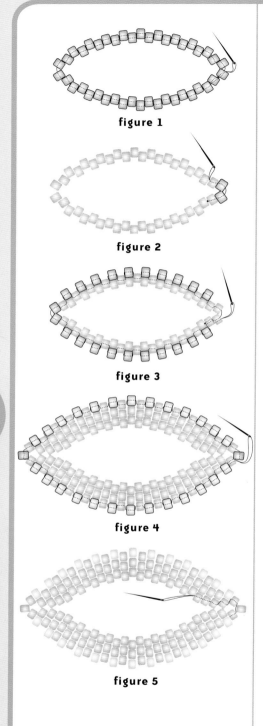

figure 1

figure 2

figure 3

figure 4

figure 5

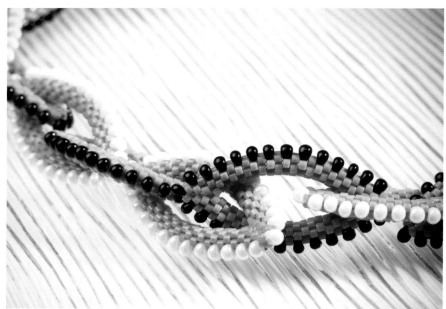

Pointed Oval Links Necklace in turquoise and orange (see page 97 for instructions on linking ovals) with black and white edge accents

These instructions are for a 20-inch (51 cm) necklace with 26 links.

▶ First Layer

With 2¼ yds (2.1 m) of thread in the needle, bring the ends together, wax well, knot, clip the tail, and melt the ends slightly.

Row 1: Pick up 1 A, 17 B, 4 A, 17 B and 3 A and form a ring secured with a lark's head knot (see page 15). Pass back through the last bead strung. Orient the work so you're working counter-clockwise (lefties, work clockwise) and work with medium tension (figure 1).

Row 2: Add 2 A and pass through the next A (don't skip a bead) (figure 2).

Peyote 10 with B. Add 2 A and pass through the next A. Peyote 10 with B. Step up (figure 3).

Rows 3 and 4: Peyote around with B but add 2 A between the pair of A beads at each point.

Row 5: Peyote around with C, but add only 1 C between the pair of A beads at each point (figure 4). This row may be worked with A if desired.

For a single-layer pointed oval, stop now, weave in the thread and trim.

▶ Second Layer

Weave through the A beads as shown so the thread exits the first A on the first inner row of the pointed oval (figure 5).

Row 1: *Peyote 9 with B. After exiting the A, add 2 A and pass through the A across from it.* Repeat from * to * once. Step up. Note that the point where the step-up occurs will move to the left. Don't miss it!

Rows 2-4: Peyote around with B but add 2 A between the pair of A beads at each point. Step up at the end of each row.

(continued on page 97)

This 19-inch (48.5 cm) necklace has 13 double-layer links joined point to point with round 4-mm fire polished glass beads. The links have 15 B beads on each side in the beginning row instead of 17. The necklace closes with a metal toggle clasp.

**Floral Motif
Necklace
composed of
single-layer
pointed ovals**

Pointed Oval Earrings in bronze with cubic zirconium double-drilled topaz oval beads inset

figure 6

Pointed Oval Earrings in bright rainbow colors

Zip the row just completed to the last row of the first layer (see page 16). At each corner, pass through the first A at the corner of the second layer, then through the single A at the corner of the first layer, and then through the second A of the second layer.

Weave in the thread and trim.

Linked Ovals
(see photo on page 94)

To connect ovals like a chain, pick up beads for a second oval, but before joining the thread for the beginning row, pass the beads through the first oval, and then join and proceed as for the first oval.

To connect single or double layer ovals point to point, join them as shown in figure 6. The extra bead between the links is optional.

Pointed Oval Earrings with black and white strips, red increases, and turquoise edge accents

PURSES

These diminutive purses are irresistible both because they're adorable and because they're so simple to make. The necklace back bars, which form the purse hardware, come in many designs and may suggest a certain style of purse to make. Simply make a flat hexagon, fold it in half, embellish it, and sew a back bar to the top before zipping the sides closed. *Voilà.*

With 2 yd (1.8 m) of thread in the needle, bring ends together, wax well, knot, clip the tail, and melt the ends slightly. **Note:** Work with very soft tension so you'll be able to fold the hexagon in half later.

Rows 1-5: Work rows 1-5 of the Basic Hexagon (see page 24).

Rows 16-20: Repeat rows 3-5 five more times. Sew the necklace back bar to one side of the hexagon (figure 1). Sew nailheads, including faux bezels with size 15° seed beads, if desired, to the outside of the hexagon. Add connector beads to one side of the hexagon next to the back bar. Fold the hexagon so the holes on the back bar are on the inside and zip the sides together (see page 16). Continue to add connector beads to the top side of the folded hexagon and the remaining side. Zip these sides together. Weave in the thread and trim.

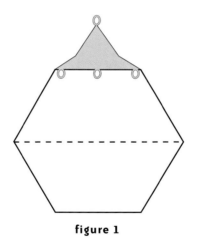

figure 1

Necklace back bars come in a variety of designs.

SUPPLIES FOR ONE 1¼-INCH (3.2CM) PURSE

Basic Beading Kit (see page 14)

Size 11° cylinder beads:
    color A, 2 g
    color B, 3 g

Size 15° seed beads (optional)

3-hole necklace back bar, 15 mm wide

Nailheads (flat-backed beads), any shape (optional)

TRILLIUM NECKLACE

A walk in the woods in early spring may afford a glimpse of this delicate wild-flower, its three oval petals alternating with three flaring pointed sepals. The real flowers bloom in white and red, pink, pale yellow, and deep maroon, but make your trilliums any color you choose. Assemble them into a lovely necklace or bracelet, or use them singly as earrings.

SUPPLIES

Basic Beading Kit (see page 14)

Size 11° cylinder beads:
    Petals: color A, 10 g; color B, 15 g
    Leaves: color A, 10 g; color B, 15 g
    15 green or yellow beads
    for the petal centers

11 round beads, 3 mm

10 to 12 inches (4 to 12 mm) of
beads for the necklace

Clasp

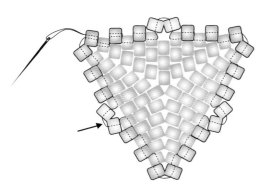

figure 1

These instructions are for an 18-inch (45.7 cm) necklace with five flowers.

▶ **Petals**

With 2 yd (1.8 m) of thread in the needle, bring the ends together, wax well, knot, clip the tail, and melt the ends slightly.

Rows 1-6: Follow instructions for the Basic Triangle, adding 2 A beads at each corner for all rows.

Row 7: *Add 2 A and pass through the next A at the corner (corner increase). Peyote 2 with B. Add 2 A and pass through the next B. This is a mid-row increase; see arrow in figure 1. Peyote 2 with B.* Repeat from * to * two more times. Step up.

(continued on page 103)

Rows 8-12: (See chart at right for number of beads for each size trillium.) Work as for row 7 but for each row, peyote one more with B between the corner increase and the mid-row increase. Be sure not to miss adding a B just before and after the mid-row increase. Allow the area of mid-row increase to curl up. Keep tension soft.

Final Row: Work as for row 7 but add only 1 A bead at each corner and at each mid-row increase instead of 2.

To draw the mid-row increases together in the center, weave through the beadwork from the corner A so the thread exits the nearest mid-row A in the last row. Pass through the remaining 2 mid-row A beads and the first mid-row A again. *Add 1 green or yellow cylinder bead and pass through the next mid-row A.* Repeat from * to * two more times. Weave in the thread and trim.

▷ Leaves

Follow the directions for the basic triangle. Work with leaf colors A and B for the number of beads specified in the chart, then work the last row with 1 A at each corner.

Weave through the beadwork to the center of the leaf and sew the leaf to the bottom of the petals with the leaf points centered between the flower petals. Weave in the thread and trim.

▷ Joining Trilliums

Make trillium petals and leaves in various graduated sizes as shown in the chart and join the tips with a 3-mm bead between them. With thread anchored and exiting the tip bead of a trillium petal, add one

figure 2

3-mm round bead. Pass through the tip bead of the next trillium, then back through the 3-mm bead and into the first tip bead from the opposite side (figure 2). Repeat. Weave in the thread and trim.

▷ Stringing the Necklace

With double thread anchored and exiting a tip bead of a trillium flower, add one 3-mm bead and half the necklace beads (5 to 6 inches [12.7 to 15.2 cm]). Pass through one side of the clasp, then back through the necklace beads and into the tip bead of the flower from the opposite side. Repeat to reinforce. Knot the thread between the beads, weave in the tail, and trim. Repeat for the other side.

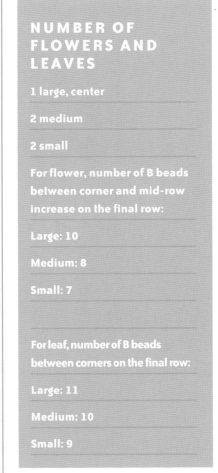

NUMBER OF FLOWERS AND LEAVES

1 large, center

2 medium

2 small

For flower, number of B beads between corner and mid-row increase on the final row:

Large: 10

Medium: 8

Small: 7

For leaf, number of B beads between corners on the final row:

Large: 11

Medium: 10

Small: 9

BAUBLE

This bauble looks complicated, but as you make it, you'll immediately see how simple it is. Friends have told me it reminds them of the headgear worn by the sisters in the old television program *The Flying Nun*; with its winged appendages, it looks like it might take to the air at any moment. Who knows what flights of fancy this bead may lead you to?

Thread a needle with 3 yd (2.7 m) of thread. Bring the ends together, wax well, knot, clip the tails, and melt with a lighter.

Rows 1-6: Follow instructions for the Basic Triangle (see page 20). Add 2 A at each corner on row 6.

Row 7: *Add 2 A and pass through the next A at the corner (corner increase). Peyote 2 with B. Add 2 A and pass through the next B (this is a mid-row increase). Peyote 2 with B.* Repeat from * to * to two more times. Step up.

Row 8: *Add 2 A and pass through the next A at the corner. Peyote 3 with B. (Thread exits the first increase A.) Add 2 A and pass through the next A of the mid-row increase. Peyote 3 with B.* Repeat from * to * two more times. Step up. **Note:** Be sure not to miss adding a B just before and after each mid-row increase. The area of increase will begin to curl up. Keep tension soft (figure 1).

Row 9: *Add 2 A and pass through the next A at the corner. Peyote 4 with B.* (Thread exits the first increase A.) Repeat from * to * two more times. Step up.

Row 10: Continue to peyote along the sides, increase at the corners and mid-row, and do a second mid-row increase

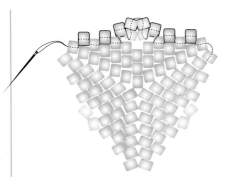

figure 1

between the corners and the first mid-row increases. There are now 12 increases on each row: the increases that form the corners of the triangle, the first mid-row increases (there are three of these) and the second mid-row increases, which are between the mid-row increases and the corners (there are six of these).

Rows 11-23: Continue to peyote around, increasing at each of the 12 increase points.

Last Row: Work peyote around but add only 1 A bead at each corner and at each first mid-row increase and at each secondary mid-row increase.

Bring the tips of the first set of corners together and join by passing through the three tip beads. Bring the tips of the third

set of corners together and join. The corners of the first set of mid-row increases will extend from the sides. Weave in the thread and trim. Add a loop of beads at the top and other accent beads at the bottom if desired.

SUPPLIES FOR ONE BAUBLE

Basic Beading Kit (see page 14)

Size 11° cylinder beads:
  color A, 3 g
  color B, 5 g

Other beads or rings as desired

STAR LOCKET

Place a photo of a loved one in this five-sided locket with scalloped edge and you've got a very special and personal piece of jewelry destined to become a family heirloom. You can glue a flat-backed round cabochon to the front of the locket for added embellishment, and a presentation pouch completes the package.

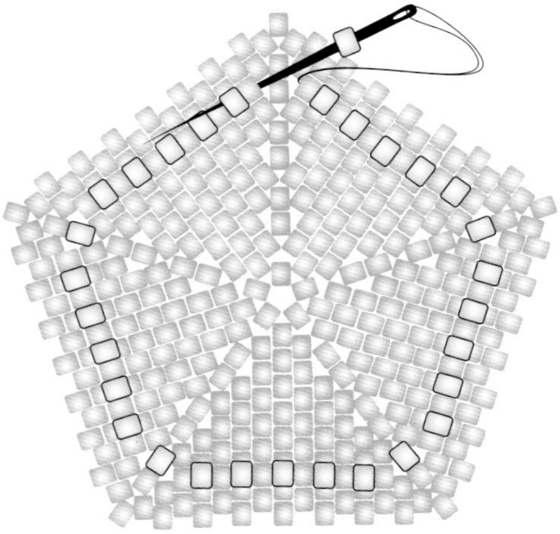

figure 1

▶ **Pentagons**

Rows 1-12: Follow instructions for the Basic Pentagon (see page 23), rows 1-12.

Rows 13-20: Repeat rows 9-12 two times.

Row 21: Repeat row 9 with all A.

Row 22: Repeat row 10 with all A.

Row 23: Repeat row 11 with A for the corner increases and B for the sides.

Row 24: Repeat row 12 with all A.

Row 25: Repeat row 9 with A for the corner increases and B for the sides.

Row 26: Repeat row 10 with all A.

Row 27: Repeat row 11 with all A.

Row 28: *Add 1 A, pass through the next 3 beads in the rows below.* Repeat from * to * around the locket with 1 A between the pairs of A at each corner.

▶ **Sides**

Locket Front: Make the first row of the picture frame as follows: Weave through the beadwork from the outer edge to the ninth row back (row 19). Work peyote upward from the pentagon to form the sides with color A (figure 1), stepping up

(continued on page 109)

SUPPLIES

Basic Beading Kit (see page 14)

Size 11° cylinder beads:
    color A, 12 g
    color B, 12 g

Round, flat-back cabochon, 14 mm (optional)

Photo laminating sheet, gloss finish, 2.5 x 3.5 inches (6.5 x 8.9 cm)

Double-sided tape

8 accent beads, 4 or 6 mm

Velvet pouch, about 3 x 4 inches (7.6 x 10.2 cm)

at the end of each row. Don't increase at the corners. Continue with even-count peyote for four more rows without increasing.

Locket Back: Follow instructions for locket front, but begin to form the sides on row 17 (the eleventh row back from the outer edge). Work three side rows, insert the picture (see Add the Picture), then decrease one bead at each corner on the last row to hold the picture in place. Knot the thread between the beads, weave in the tail, and trim.

▶ Tassel

Attach the tassel to the bottom point of the locket front before joining the front to the back.

With 1 yd (0.9 m) of single thread in the needle, anchor the thread so it exits the center bead at the bottom of the front pentagon. Add 8 A, one 4- or 6-mm bead, 12 A or B, one 4- or 6-mm bead, and 1 A. Skipping the last bead, pass back through all the beads on the string and the bead exited in the pentagon from the opposite side.

Add 7 A or B and pass through the eighth bead on the beginning string and the 4- or 6-mm bead, then add 15 A or B, a 4- or 6-mm bead and 1 A. Skipping the last bead, pass back through all the beads strung, anchoring again in the pentagon bead. Complete three more strands this way, each three beads longer than the previous strand. Don't cut the thread.

▶ Attach the Front to the Back

Continuing with the thread from the tassel, weave through to the bottom corner bead on the edge of the frame and then through the bottom corner bead on the frame of the locket back. Reinforce a few times, weave in the thread and trim.

▶ Add the Picture

Trim the photo to fit the five-sided shape and embed it in the laminating sheet following the manufacturer's instructions. Trim the edges ⅛ inch (3 mm) away from the photo edge, rounding the corners slightly. Apply double-sided tape to the back of the laminated photo and press into the locket back.

▶ Closure

Sew a small button or bead to the center top of the locket back and attach a loop of beads large enough to fit over the button to the locket front.

▶ Chain

Following the instructions on page 115, make a diagonal stripe chain 25 inches (63.5 cm) long or to your desired length for use without a clasp. Attach to the locket corners with an accent bead.

▶ Optional Locket Presentation Pouch

Make a smaller version of the locket front by working rows 1-12 and then rows 26-28. Sew this motif to the front of the drawstring pouch and embellish with other beads as desired.

QUICK REFERENCE

Use the following three pages as a quick reference for making the various peyote increases for basic shapes. *Note:* **Remember to step-up at the end of every row. Watch for it!**

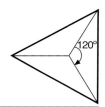

Triangle

Row 1: Tie 3 A in a circle. Pass through 1 bead.

Row 2: Add 2 A and pass through the next bead (don't skip a bead). Repeat two more times.

Row 3: Add 2 A and pass through the next A (don't skip a bead) at each corner and peyote the sides with B.

Repeat row 3 to desired size.

Final Row (optional): Add 1 A bead at each corner.

This Silver Triangle Pin with channel-set stone embellishments and drop crystal pendant uses the basic peyote stitch and triangle increase.

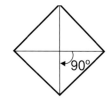

Square

Row 1: Tie 4 A in a circle. Pass through 1 bead.

Row 2: Add 1 B and pass through the next bead (don't skip a bead). Repeat three more times.

Row 3: Add 3 A at each corner. Push the center bead down so it touches the bead in the row below.

Row 4: Add 2 A at each corner as follows: after exiting the first A of the three at the corner in the previous row, add 2 A and pass through the third A. Peyote the sides with B.

Row 5: Add 2 A at each corner. Peyote the sides with B.

Row 6: Add 1 A between the two A at each corner. Peyote the sides with B.

Row 7: Peyote around with B.

Repeat rows 3-7 to desired size, ending with row 6.

This necklace uses the basic peyote stitch for the square.

This Star Locket uses the pentagon shape.

Pentagon

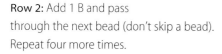

Row 1: Tie 5 A in a circle. Pass through 1 bead.

Row 2: Add 1 B and pass through the next bead (don't skip a bead). Repeat four more times.

Row 3: Add 2 A and pass through the next bead. Repeat four more times. (These pairs form the *V* at each corner.)

Row 4: Peyote around with B adding 1 A between the pair of A beads at each corner.

Row 5: Peyote around with B.

Row 6: Add 3 A at each corner. (Push the

center bead down so it touches the bead in the row below.) Peyote the sides with B.

Row 7: Add 2 A at each corner as follows: After exiting the first A of the three at the corner in the previous row, add 2 A and pass through the third A. Peyote the sides with B.

Repeat rows 4-7 to desired size, ending with row 4.

Hexagon

Row 1: Tie 6 A in a circle. Pass through 1 bead.

Row 2: Add 1 A and pass through the next bead (don't skip a bead). Repeat five more

times. These A beads are the corners of the hexagon.

Row 3: Peyote around with B.

Row 4: Add 2 A and pass through the next B. Repeat five more times.

Row 5: Add 1 A between the 2 A at each corner. Peyote the sides with B.

Row 6: Peyote around with B.

Row 7: Add 2 A above the A at each corner. Peyote the sides with B.

Repeat rows 5-7 to desired size, ending with row 5.

ADDITIONAL STITCHES

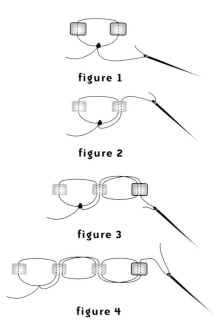

figure 1

figure 2

figure 3

figure 4

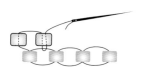

figure 5

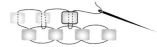

figure 6

figure 7

Single-Needle Ladder Stitch

1. Pick up 2 beads. Knot the working thread to the tail with a square knot (figure 1).

2. Pass through the bead on the right (figure 2).

3. Add 1 bead. Pass up through the previous bead and down through the new bead (figure 3).

4. Add 1 bead. Pass down through the previous bead and up through the new bead (figure 4).

Repeat steps 3 and 4 for the desired length.

Brick Stitch

Row 1: Work a single-needle ladder of the desired length for the base row.

Row 2: With thread exiting the top of a bead in the base row (or existing row), add 2 beads, pass the needle under the thread between the last two beads in the previous row, then pass back up through the last bead (figure 5).

To continue across the row, add 1 bead, pass the needle under the thread between the next two beads in the previous row, then pass back up through the last bead added (figure 6).

Increase at the End of Row

After passing back up through the last bead, add a second bead connected like the previous bead (figure 7).

Square Stitch

1. Pick up 4 beads. Tie the thread with a square knot to form a ring (figure 8).

2. Pass back through the last 2 beads (figure 9).

3. Add 2 beads. Pass back through the bead next to the bead the thread exits (figure 10).

4. Pass through the bead above and the first of the two new beads (figure 11).

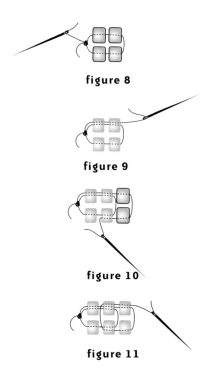

figure 8

figure 9

figure 10

figure 11

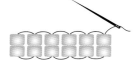

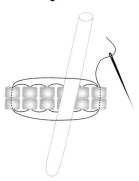

figure 12

figure 13

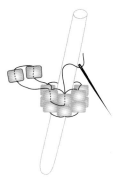

figure 14

figure 15

Herringbone Chain

This herringbone chain is worked with size 11° cylinder beads around 3-mm satin cord (also known as rattail cord), which provides support and prevents the chain from stretching. A beginning row of six beads fits nicely around the cord.

Base Row: Leaving an 8-inch (20.3 cm) tail, make a single-needle ladder 2 beads wide and 6 beads long (figure 12).

With thread exiting the top right of the ladder, lay the cord on the ladder and connect the ends of the ladder. Pass down through the 2 beads on the left and up through the last 2 beads on the right (figure 13). Pull tight to join the ends (figure 14).

Row 1: *Add 2 beads. Pass down through the bead next to the bead just exited, then up through the bead next to that one (figure 15). * Repeat from * to * two more times. On the last repeat, step up by passing through the first bead added in this row.

Repeat this row for desired length. With a new thread, wrap one end of the satin cord with thread and stitch through it to bind the end and prevent fraying. Sew the end of the beadwork to the end of the cord. Add a bead cap, a small bead, and one end of a clasp. Pass back through the bead and the bead cap. Stitch into the satin cord. Repeat to reinforce. Repeat with on the other end.

Diagonal Stripe Chain

Work with round seed beads or cylinder beads in two colors, dark and light. Keep your tension tight. The key to success with this chain is pulling the thread in the proper direction. The arrow in the illustration indicates the direction to pull the thread.

1. With 3 yd (2.7 m) of thread in the needle, bring ends together and wax well. Leaving a 6-inch (15.2 cm) tail, tie 1 light bead on the end of the thread (figure 16).

2. Add 3 dark beads and 3 light beads. Pass back through the tied-on bead (figure 17).

3. Draw this into a loop as illustrated in figure 18.

4. Add 3 dark beads and pass through the fifth bead strung in the beginning loop (figure 19).

5. Add 2 light beads and 3 dark beads and pass back through the second bead counting back from where the needle exits a bead (figure 20).

6. Add 3 light beads and pass through the fourth bead, again counting the bead the thread exits as number one (figure 21).

7. Add 2 dark beads and 3 light beads and pass back through the second bead as in step 5 (figure 22).

8. Add 3 dark beads and pass through the fourth bead as in step 6 (figure 23).

Repeat steps 5-8 until the chain is desired length.

figure 16

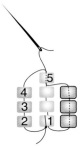

figure 17

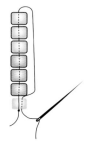

figure 18

figure 19

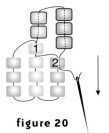

figure 20

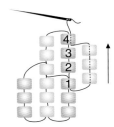

figure 21

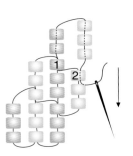

figure 22

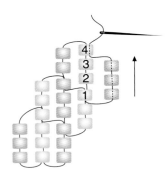

figure 23

115

ABOUT THE AUTHOR

Diane Fitzgerald is a bead jewelry designer who works with a variety of beads, large and small, old and new. Since 1989, she's taught bead classes across the United States and internationally. Her travels have taken her to South Africa to study Zulu beadwork and to the Czech Republic, Germany, and Japan to learn about the glass bead industry and meet bead workers and bead makers. This is Diane's tenth book, and she has authored numerous magazine articles devoted to beads and beadwork.

Diane is a featured artist in Lark Books' *Masters: Beadweaving*. She was the 2008 recipient of the Bead & Button Show Excellence in Bead Artistry Award and was once voted one of the top five beading teachers by readers of *Beadwork* magazine. She loves helping people with their beadweaving and welcomes questions. To get in touch with her, visit her website, dianefitzgerald.com, or email her at dmfbeads@bitstream.net.

ACKNOWLEDGMENTS

Many thanks to all my students who have given me feedback on the projects, pointed out flaws in my instructions, and urged me onward.

Thanks, too, to the staff of Lark Books, especially Nathalie Mornu and Ray Hemachandra, who made this book a smooth and pleasant production. I'm grateful to Dana Irwin for her spot-on art direction and to Kathleen McCafferty, editorial interns Katie Henderson and Courtney Metz, art production assistant Bradley Norris, and junior designer Carol Morse for keeping the book on track.

Thanks to J'aime Allene for her beautiful illustrations and to Lynne Harty for her gorgeous photographs; and last, but surely not least, thanks to Judith Durant, my faithful and trusted editor, who struggles so patiently with me.

It's all on www.larkbooks.com

Can't find the materials you need to create a project?
Search our database for craft suppliers & sources for hard-to-find materials.

Got an idea for a book?
Read our book proposal guidelines and contact us.

Want to show off your work?
Browse current calls for entries.

Want to know what new and exciting books we're working on?
Sign up for our free e-newsletter.

Feeling crafty?
Find free, downloadable project directions on the site.

Interested in learning more about the authors, designers & editors who create Lark books?

117

INDEX